Canine Animal Assisted Therapy For Children With Autism Spectrum Disorder:

A Guideline to Program Development and Therapeutic Intervention

Renee Farneti Jensen

Published by Carol Farneti Foster in cooperation with Goatslug Publications.

Goatslug Publications
1128 Gritter Ridge Rd.
Stanton, KY 40380
Email: theroguebiologist@gmail.com

Printed in the USA by Lightning Source.

ISBN: 978-0-9998023-7-3

T

This book is dedicated to Vicki, the extraordinary therapy dog, who helped change the lives of many children diagnosed with Autism Spectrum Disorder

TABLE OF CONTENTS

      Brief History of Animal Therapy
      Animal Assisted Activities (AAA) vs. Animal Assisted Therapy (AAT)
      Research on Children Within the Autistic Spectrum & AAT
      General Benefits
      Choosing a Certified Dog Trainer
      Choosing an Appropriate Dog
      Helpful Hints During Training
      Introducing Vicki and Her Special Tricks
      Choosing a Facility
      Choosing a Canine Assisted Therapy (AAT) Team
      Educating Staff
      Liability Insurance-National or State
      Documentation
      Children who may not benefit for animal assisted therapy (AAT)
      Zoonotic prevention and precautions
      Recommended facility requirements
      Group and individual treatment options
      The Developmental, Individual-Difference, (DID)
      Relationship-Based : The Floor Time Approach
      Sensory Integration
      The Miller Method: A Cognitive-Developmental Systems Approach
      Applied Behavioral Analysis (ABA)
      Individual treatment goals and activities
      Group treatment goals
      Group theme activities
      Classroom group activities
      Input from Renee and Vicki

APPENDICES

ACKNOWLEDGEMENTS

It has always been my goal to publish an Occupational Therapy book, however, I was unclear about the subject. Due to a medical illness, my life has led me down the exciting, unique Occupational Therapy pathway of writing! Hence, I feel very passionate about helping children on the autistic spectrum and my love of dogs. Combining my two passions led me to write about helping children with Autism Spectrum Disorder, ASD using Animal Assisted Therapy (AAT). Throughout the writing process, I have many people to thank. Without their patience, love, and guidance this book would have not become a reality.

I would like to thank:
My family, Robert and Aleacia Jensen, my husband and daughter, who inspired me to work toward my dream. Their support and love are the most important aspects of my life.

My friend Rebecca Lugara, a writer herself who has encouraged me along the way to continue writing even when I felt discouraged. I am grateful to her for taking time out of her busy schedule to endlessly read and edit my book.

My niece, Amy Bennett a certified dog trainer at New Hope Assistance Dogs, Warren, Pennsylvania https://www.newhopedogs.net. who I can call anytime for advice and for giving me Vicki. She introduced me to the certified animal therapy dog world and let me observe her in a hospital setting with her faithful dog, Shadow.

My friend, Wendy Elmo, an author and a speech language pathologist, who has inspired me from the first day I met her. Wendy's enthusiasm and positive energy has provided me to forge into completing this book.

A special thanks also to Nichole McDowell and Michelle Mead for letting Vicki and I work with the children of their preschool program.

~Renee

This book was originally written prior to the author's death in 2011. Since her passing, the book has been reviewed and updated with recent research to support her strategies by Donna Kelly and Rebecca Thorne Lugar. Renee's family wishes to express their deep gratitude to these two ladies.

It was Renee's dying wish that her life's work and passion be published to support the lives of children and parents who fall within the autism spectrum. Her sister, Carol Farneti Foster, has worked alongside Judy Dourson of Goatslug Publications to fulfill this request. Thanks to everyone involved in this process.

Vicki's Introduction

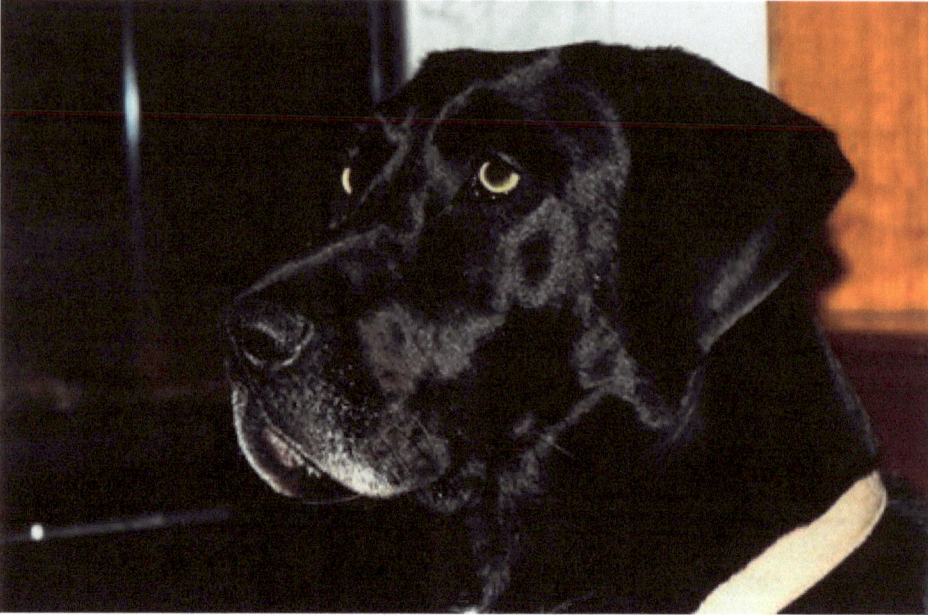

Hi, my name is Vicki. I am a black Labrador Retriever and Great Dane mix. Since there is a Labradoodle I suppose you can call me a Labradane or a Great Lab. I must keep up with the fashionable names. Aren't I a cool mixed breed? I am a therapy dog at an autistic spectrum preschool. I hear the children now… "Hey Vicki's here!" "Vicki's here to see me!" "Hey guys!"

I wag my sleek, jet-black tail and frolic toward the delightful children to say hello. The children run up to pet and "chat" with me.

I am thinking, "I will come back to get you after you settle in your classroom"

I wait patiently and walk away, looking forward to seeing the children again.

Let me tell you a little about what I do at this preschool.

My owner, Renee, and I come to visit my special friends several times a month. My friends and co-workers (the professional staff) devise the children's therapy goals. Then Renee and my coworkers come up with fun and creative ideas to meet the children's goals using me as the therapeutic modality. Me, as a therapeutic modality! Doesn't that sound impressive? As the therapeutic modality (HEE HEE)

I get to have fun playing with the children in each session. I must say the activities are interesting. I do look rather dashing when I wear my plaid red shirt, red t-shirt, green necklace and headband during dress up time with the children.

Renee and I must be going to meet our first child in his classroom. Renee will explain more of the details later. We are off to have some fun! It was nice chatting with you! ~Vicki.

Renee's Introduction

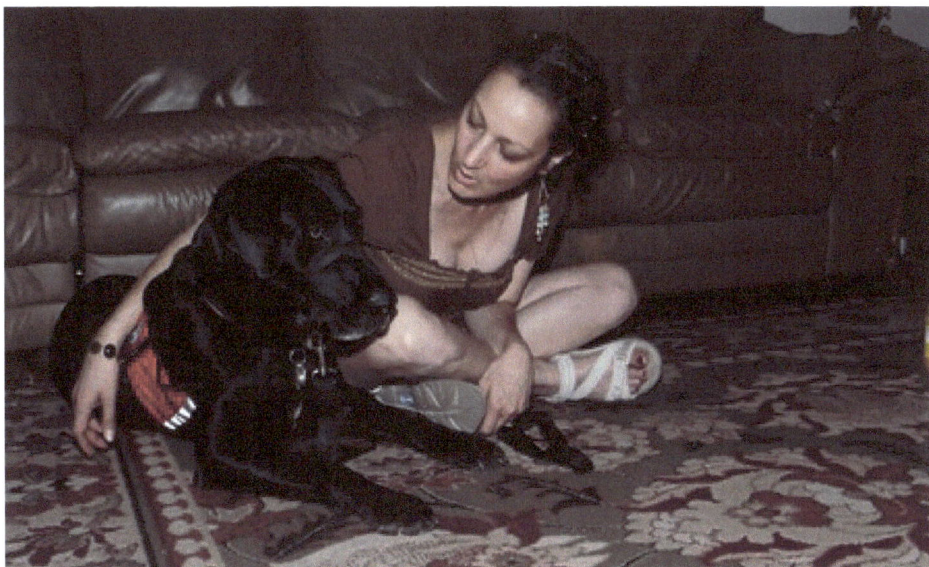

Vicki sure has a "way with words". Vicki is a great listener, doesn't talk back, is non-judgmental, and is always happy to see the children. Can you say that about most of the people you see everyday?

Dogs and humans have been companions throughout history. Vicki has proven herself a great companion to me during a time of medical illness. So why shouldn't Vicki help others? Combining my Occupational Therapy background, and love of dogs, I realized why not train Vicki to become an Animal Assistive Therapy dog to help children on the autistic spectrum? Now my dream is a reality!

Congratulations! If you have reached this point successfully, you have found a dog that is a great candidate!

The tests are strict because your dog must be even-tempered and adaptable. Working with young children has special rewards and hurdles. There must be no doubt in your mind that your dog shows no tendency toward aggression, can be trusted, and is loving and affectionate.

Training Your Dog
We have the trainer and the dog, now it is training time! Bernard-Curran et al. (2008), DVD, suggests puppy or dog proofing your home. In the video, she and her colleagues discuss proper dog crates and crating, and suggest household "do's and don'ts."

Prior to beginning your training, thoroughly investigate a dog certification program. Once chosen, contact the certification dog program and sign up for its obedience classes. Prior to the class, contact the specific obedience trainer and ask questions (noted above). Bernard-Curran et al. (2008) states formal obedience training should begin by sixteen weeks, the point at which all immunizations are given.

In the obedience class, the trainer will teach you how to train your dog to follow commands and how to socialize your dog. The most common commands are, "sit," "down," "stay," "heel," and "come"; however, other commands can also be incorporated.

Helpful Hints During Training
Now that you have your puppy or dog, be prepared to put many hours aside for bonding and training. In addition to completing the trainer's suggestions from class, you can complete additional tasks while playing with your dog. Some additional hints regarding training:

Touch is an important ongoing aspect of any therapy dog's training. Bernard-Curran (2008) and Amy Bennett (pers. comm., 2008) recommends touching and handling the dog several times a day. During quiet times, pet your dog lightly; tug on his ears, tail, collar, mouth, and fur over all body parts. Give the dog a gentle but restraining hug and use him as a pillow or place or your supported weight on him. Always make sure you are the one who ends the touching session by stopping the petting and getting up and walking away.

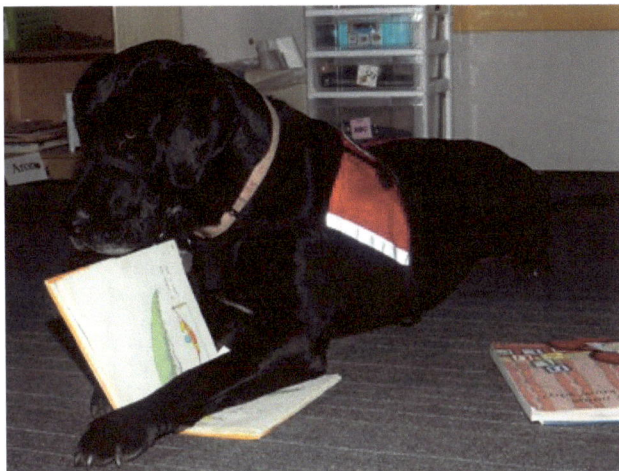

Off we went with the help of my niece, Amy, a professional service dog trainer, and with her advice, we went to obedience training; to learn tricks, and to get certified. After investigation, we found a preschool program where Vicki and I joined the rehabilitation team. We worked hard on impressing our new colleagues by being on our best behavior, meeting the facility administration, and speaking to the professional staff about Animal Assistive Therapy. We developed an Animal Assistive Therapy program by researching and devising creative activities. "We ladies" put on quite a show… and now we are a successful certified dog therapy team!

Vicki and I put so much hard work into our endeavor that we decided to form a certified therapy team to assist others by writing a book. This book which is based on professional and personal experiences, contains invaluable information, general guidelines, and reproducible information.

Being "ladies of the millennium", with family and work commitments, we realize that time is of the essence; so why reinvent the wheel? We have done the work you will need to become a certified therapy team working with children with special needs. The rewards are PRICELESS!

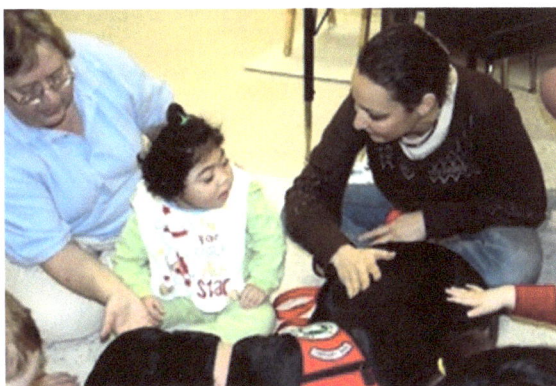

Chapter 1: Populations That Could Benefit from Animal Assisted Therapy

This chapter begins with an overall view of populations that can and do benefit from Animal Assisted therapies. This book however focuses on children with autistic spectrum disorder (ASD).

According to research done by Morrison (2012), Animal Assisted Interventions (AAI) have been reported to have statistically significant beneficial effects for improvements in many areas including heart rate, blood pressure, depression, anxiety, and loneliness. There is a need to do more research in this field to support the use of Animal Assisted therapies and the populations that they could serve.

There have been animal assisted therapies since the Ninth Century through the present day. Typically, the populations served began with the mentally ill in the 1700's, epilepsy patients in the 1800's, blood pressure patients in the 1970's, and nursing homes (Morrison, 2012). Most of the research that has been done over the years has been focused in the psychology field, even though other disciplines and diagnoses have benefited from this form of therapy.

There are a growing amount of professionals who are using animal assisted therapy within the classroom, therapy sessions, and a variety of facilities and diagnoses. These include nurses, psychologists, social workers; and speech, occupational, and physical therapists, (Kruger & Serpell, 2006). Recently, and within this book, the focus of Animal Assisted Therapy)(AAT) has been related to goal-directed therapy intervention and more specifically with a dog, Vicki. Occupational therapy functional goals for children or adults with various disabilities and health care issues are being used in combination with Animal Assisted Therapy. Occupational therapists are presently using AAT in many therapy clinics, schools, and facilities throughout the world and working with a variety of diagnoses including children and adults with cerebral palsy, strokes, muscle diseases, mental illness, veterans, emotional issues, and autism spectrum disorder.

Autistic Spectrum Disorder Clinical Observations

Children with Autism Spectrum Disorder or ASD have difficulty with social interaction, communication, and patterns of behavior. The child on the autism spectrum may present with impairments in sensory integration, cognition, vision, gross and fine motor skills, and everyday life tasks. It should be noted that not all the impairments for these children are mentioned here, as it is beyond the scope of this book.

In very general terms, sensory integration is the ability to take in information from the senses (vision, smell, touch, auditory, taste, vestibular, and muscles and joints), process the information and then appropriately react to the environment. Some sensory integration difficulties may include pushing and grabbing others, spinning, hand flapping, humming, aversion to smells, difficulty with touching and food textures, head tilting, delayed auditory processing, covering ears in response to loud noises, and not responding to his or her name.

The term "cognition" refers to knowing or thinking. Children with ASD may display difficulty with attention span, following directions, safety, impulsivity and judgment.

Gross and fine motor skills are also affected. In general, gross motor skills are the larger movements of arms, legs, feet, or the entire body; fine motor skills are the smaller movements of the hand and fingers. Difficulty with gross motor skills may include difficulty in running, jumping, riding a bike, and hopping. Difficulty with fine motor skills may include picking up small objects, holding a pencil correctly, and writing. Both gross motor and fine motor skills can be affected due to poor motor planning.

Motor planning is the initiation, performance and execution of a series of movements. Motor planning difficulties can be seen with any motor task. An example of poor motor planning is when the child has difficulty with moving or lifting his or her leg to mount a bicycle, and peddle once he or she is sitting on a bicycle; or form letters to write his name or words, etc.

J. A. Ayres (2000) states that vision and visual perceptual difficulties are also prevalent among children who were at that time diagnosed with Autism. Some observable visual problems are poor eye contact, deceased visual attention, clumsiness, visual fixation on a toy for long periods of time, and distractibility. Some observable visual perception difficulties are stacking blocks, putting puzzles together, getting lost, drawing, distinguishing pattern designs, telling the foreground from background of a picture, or writing between the lines.

Activities of Daily Living (ADLs) are everyday life skills, which include feeding, grooming, dressing, bathing, playing and academics. Children with ASD may have difficulties with some or all of these everyday life activities.

Children with ASD also display a variety of behavioral problems; however, these descriptions are well beyond the scope of this book. For the purpose of this publication these behavioral issues, such as aggression towards others and animals, may eliminate the child's ability from participation in the Animal Assisted Therapy (AAT) program.

Autistic spectrum disorder remains very complex as each child is unique and presents with his or her very own strengths and needs.

Chapter 2: Animal Assisted Therapy (AAT)

Frequently asked questions:
- **When did this idea of using animals as a form of therapy begin?**
- **What is the difference between Animal Assisted Activities (AAA) and Animal Assisted Therapy (AAT)?**
- **Is there any research suggesting that AAT works?**
- **What are the benefits to AAT?**

Brief History of Animal Therapy
The York Retreat in England in 1792 used animals therapeutically in a positive way as mental illness patients learned to care for them (Burch 2003, and Cusack & Smith 1984). Florence Nightingale, in 1859, wrote that animals could be beneficial for companionship of the sick (Burch 2003). Bethel in West Germany used traditional animals, game park animals, and farm animals with patients with epilepsy and other illnesses in 1867 (Cusack & Smith 1984). St. Elizabeth's Hospital in Washington, D.C.

recorded the use of animals for psychiatric residents in 1919 (Burch, 2003). In 1942, Pawling Army Air Force Base Convalescent Hospital in New York was the first to formally use farm animals and reptiles in treating patients with fatigue and physical injury (Burch, 2003). In the 1950's, Boris Levinson, an American psychologist, happened to have his dog in his office during a consultation when an eight-year-old, non-communicative boy came in for treatment. Since the dog was of interest to the child, the boy started to play with the dog. Levinson used the dog as a modality for a breakthrough in his treatment. In the 1960's, Levinson was the first person credited with integrating animal assistive therapy into clinical psychology. Several studies have been conducted since his initial documentation of "the dog as the co-therapist" written in 1962.

Since the 1960's, a plethora of books, research, and articles have been written on Animal Therapy in many settings. Later in this book, I will share the published articles specifically on Canine Animal Assisted Therapy and Autistic Children.

Animal Assisted Activities vs. Animal Assisted Therapy
There are two types of pet facilitated therapy: Animal Assisted Activities (AAA) and Animal Assisted Therapy (AAT).

The Delta Society published the original "The Standards of Practice" in 1996, which provided the definitions used in this book of Animal Assisted Therapy as a way to establish standardized terminology in the field, (Morrison, 2012). In 1999 the Delta Society published The Standards of Practice for Animal-Assisted Activities and Therapy, (Morrison, 2012).

The Wellness Guidelines for Animals in Animal Assisted Activity (2014) definition is: Animal Assisted Therapy (AAT) "is a goal directed intervention in which an animal that meets specific criteria is an integral part of the treatment process". "AAT (2014) is designed to improve human physical, social, emotional, and cognitive (e.g. thinking and intellectual skills) function; and animals may be formally included in activities such as physical, occupational, and speech therapy.)

"Animal assisted activities (AAA), provides opportunities for motivational, educational, recreational, and/or therapeutic benefits to enhance quality of life. AAA is delivered in a variety of environments by specially trained professionals, paraprofessionals, and/or volunteers, in association with animals that meet specific criteria." (Delta Society, 2005).

During AAA, the role of the dog and its handler is to "meet and greet" adults or children in a variety of environments. These environments may include nursing homes, psychiatric hospitals, medical hospitals, and schools. During these visits, the content is spontaneous or a previous utilized activity can be repeated. The volunteer does not have to provide detailed notes or keep a formal client log as there are no specific goals to meet.

Animal assisted therapy (AAT) "is a goal-directed intervention in which an animal that meets specific criteria is an integral part of the treatment process. AAT is directed and/or delivered by a health/human service professional with specialized expertise, and within the scope of practice of his/her profession. AAT is designed to promote improvement in physical, social, emotional, and/or cognitive functioning [cognitive functioning refers to thinking and intellectual skills]. AAT is provided in a variety of settings and may be group or individual in nature. This process is documented and evaluated." (Delta Society, 2005).

The interventions can be done by a variety of trained physical and occupational therapists, and other licensed professionals, (Delta Society, 2005; Kruger & Serpell, 2006). Therapy programs are provided in a variety of settings and may involve individuals or groups. In AAT, specified goals and objectives are determined for each patient and their progress is evaluated and documented." Sometimes a term that includes both such as in Morrison (2012) reviews the literature under the collective name of Animal Assistive Interventions (AAI), which includes both Animal Assistive Activities (AAA), and Animal Assistive Therapy (AAT).

Key Features of Animal-Assisted Therapy:
- AAT is goal-directed.
- There is a specific end in mind, such as improvement in social skills, range of motion, verbal skills, and attention span.
- Any visit with an animal may result in the achievement of one or more of these goals.
- The goals are established and monitored during the treatment session.
- Each documented session goes into the person's record with the progress and activity noted.

If I were asked to sum up AAT in my own words for the purposes of this book, I would say that AAT is the use of a certified therapy dog as a creative therapeutic modality to assist children on the autistic spectrum to improve their individualized treatment goals.

Research on Children with ASD and Animal Assisted Therapy
Although many studies regarding the benefits of animal therapy are documented, there has been more research for Animal Assistive Therapy in the field of mental health, and making physiological improvements with adults and children. Kamiaoka et al. (2014) did a review of randomized controlled trials looking at the effectiveness of animal-assisted therapy, and Stewart et al. (2013) provided a review of the philosophical framework for therapists in that field. Silva et al. (2011) noted increased positive behavioral responses thought to improve the participation of a child with ASD for behavioral therapy sessions.

I will focus only on the studies I have found that specifically target AAT. Redefer & Goodman (1989) studied twelve autistic children who displayed an immediate increase in social interaction when the dog was present. The children displayed a decrease in autistic-like behaviors such as hand flapping, spinning and humming; and an increase in social behaviors such as interaction with the therapist by joining in, imitating, and initiating activities. After a one-month follow up without the dog and with an unfamiliar therapist, social interaction skills declined; however, they remained above the baseline results. The authors attribute this improvement in social behavior not only to the presence of the dog, but to the therapist's ability to assist the child in facilitating play, sustaining an activity, broadening his responses, and learning to communicate with the dog.

Martin & Farnum (2002) analyzed behavioral and verbal skills of ten children with Pervasive Developmental Disorder (PDD) using a non-social toy (ball), a stuffed dog, and a live dog. Overall, with the live dog present, the children laughed more, gave treats to the dog, displayed a more playful mood and increased energy, focused on the dog, initiated numerous conversations and exchanges with the dog, engaged in discussions with therapist regarding the dog, were more apt to agree with the therapist and were less inclined to disregard questions from the therapist. These researchers conclude that there was a positive behavioral and verbal effect on children with PDD.

On the website http://www.hamline.edu/instech/honors/erin_farrell.pdf a research study called The Effects of Animal Assisted Therapy in Children with Autism completed by Erin Farrell at Hamline University investigated the use of animal assisted therapy dogs with children on the autism spectrum in a school setting; specifically investigating Social Understanding, Social Commutation and Social Interaction. Data collection was taken on each child in an AAT environment and in a non-AAT environment. The results revealed that an AAT environment for children with ASD in a school system facilitated social communication, interaction, participation and initiation of communication.

Sams et al. (2006) did a pilot investigation of incorporating animals for children with autism. The website http://youtube.com/watch?v=nHbXVxheEL8&feature=related, provides excellent videotape presentations of a therapist treating a child with ASD in a Canine Animal Assisted Therapy Program.

General Benefits
General Benefits of Animal Assisted Activities and Animal Assisted Therapy Dogs cited on the online website, deltasociety.org and integrates general benefits with the authors' experience.

Empathy
A child with ASD may have difficulty understanding the feeling and emotions of others. Therefore, an animal (dog) may help the child in learning to be empathetic to parents, siblings, and classmates. The child sees the animal as a peer; hence, it is easier to teach the child to be empathetic with an animal than with a human. The child can learn to read an animal's body language, which will possibly carry over to daily life experience with people. The child may be able to interpret the animals' feelings, as animals are straightforward and "live in the moment."

Outward Focus
Children with ASD are frequently self-absorbed. An animal (dog) can help the child focus on his surrounding environment, as he can watch, talk to, or about the animal.

Nurturing

Because children with ASD may display a multitude of weaknesses, nurturing skills may be difficult for them to learn. A child with ASD can take care of the animal during the session. The child can get the dog food and a drink to encourage nurturing skills.

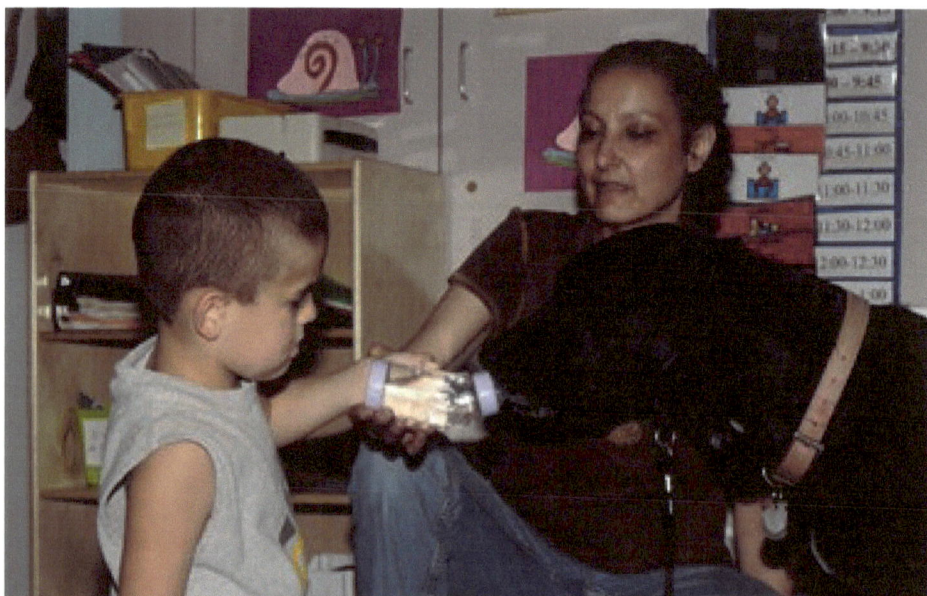

Rapport

Due to the child's social communication issues, rapport with others may be difficult. The animal (dog) may help ease transition. In a non-threatening and emotionally safe environment, the dog may facilitate communication between child, therapist, handler, and classmates.

Acceptance

A child with ASD may have had negative experiences in which they did not receive a child's or adult's approval. An animal's (dog) acceptance is nonjudgmental and forgiving.

Socialization

One of the biggest challenges the child on the autistic spectrum has is in the area of social communication. There is more laughter and interaction among residents when an animal visits a facility. This laughter and interaction encourages socialization among other children, teachers, the handler and all others involved in the session including the therapy dog.

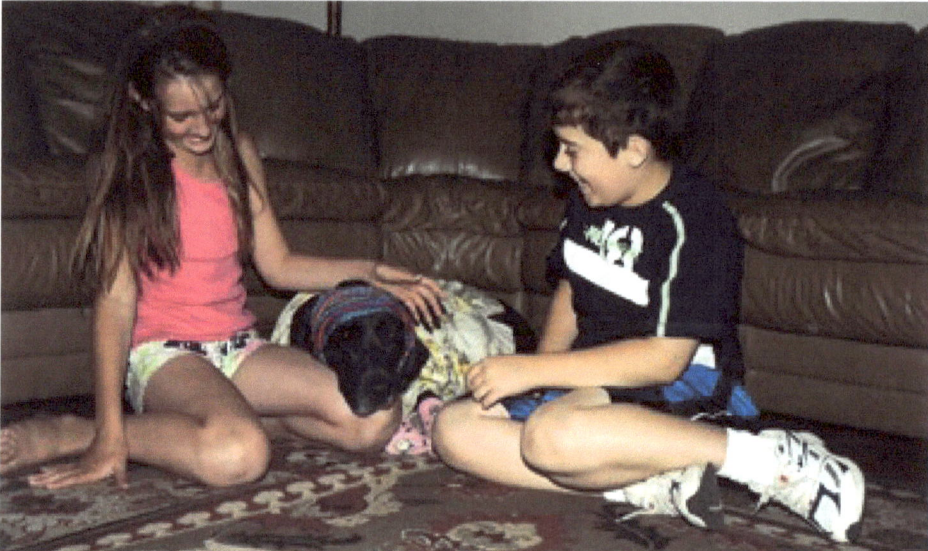

Mental Stimulation

The animal (dog) provides mental stimulation because of increased communication, laughter, play and entertainment; along with brightening up the atmosphere.

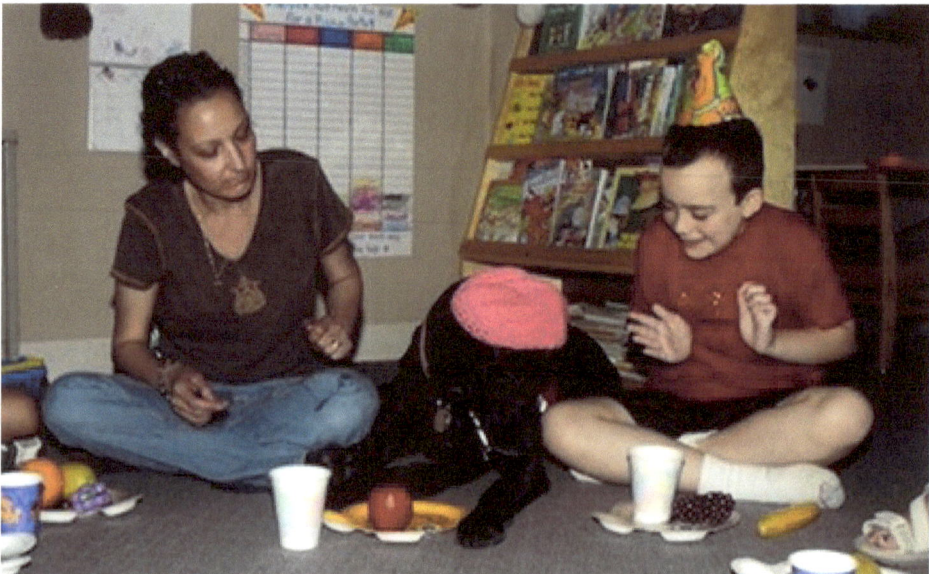

Physical Contact and Touch

The child with ASD may have difficulty with tactile stimulation which can interfere with his or her developmental process. Perhaps for some children, a dog can give an acceptable warm furry touch that a human cannot provide. An animal's touch (dog) may be safe, non-threatening, and pleasant which can serve as a stepping-stone, transitioning the child to be able to touch other textures and people.

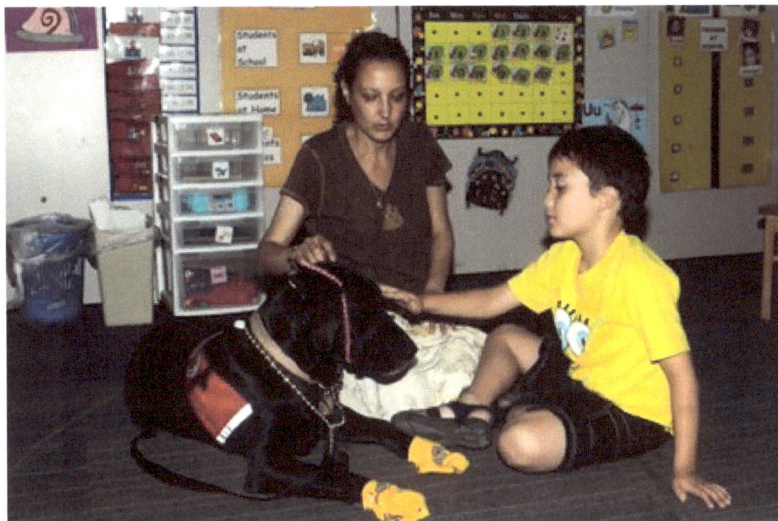

Physiological Benefits

The child with ASD may present with a lot of self-stimulatory behavior. A dog's presence can be a calming factor for the child. The therapist may want to integrate a slow rhythmic petting activity to facilitate calming of a child.

For centuries, dogs have been great companions to humans! Dogs love you unconditionally, they are happy to see you, they are easier to read emotionally than humans are, and they provide a "warm fuzzy" feeling. I believe that children with autistic spectrum may sense these wonderful dog traits and reap the benefits of AAT, and AAT. Research with children with ASD certainly has shown positive results.

Chapter 3: The Canine Assistive Therapy Dog

Animal assisted therapy dogs are carefully chosen as children with ASD may display loud and unpredictable behaviors. These special children need a calm, friendly, gentle, even-tempered dog! You want a dog to be loving, loyal, people-oriented, tolerant, and willing.

Choosing a certified dog trainer
It is recommended that you find a certified dog trainer who can assist you in choosing the correct pure breed or mixed breed puppy or dog to become a certified animal assisted therapy dog. Begin looking for a certified dog trainer at the Delta Society website **www.deltasociety.org** which lists trainers and programs throughout the USA, contact Therapy Dogs International, Inc. at **www.tdi-dog.org/default.aspx** or ask your veterinarian. When you contact the prospective trainer, you may want to ask them some specific questions.

Some questions you may want to ask the dog trainer:
• How long have you been working with therapy dogs?
• Where have you been certified?
• How long have you been certified?
• What organization are you certified by?
• Have you worked with a variety of breeds?

- In what environments have you trained dogs (parks, community places)
- Do you own a certified therapy dog? If so, what settings have you worked in?
- Do you do practice positive reinforcement training?
- Do you have experience working with children with autistic spectrum disorder?
- Are you available for one-to-one consults?
- Do you conduct obedience classes?
- Do you conduct therapy dog classes?
- May I observe one of your classes?
  While the trainer is in class, be sure to observe:
  ~His/her methods of training (positive reinforcement, praise, etc)
  ~if he or she is observant of the dog's behavior
  ~his or her interaction with the dog
  ~if he or she is clear on his or her instructions
  ~if he or she is clear on answering questions
- Can the you (the trainer) recommend additional activities to address and improve problematic dog behavior at home?

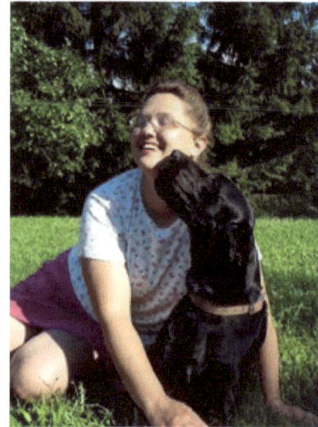

When you choose an animal assistive therapy dog, it is highly recommended that you hire someone, or ask the certification institution to assist or provide a dog trainer who is familiar with temperament testing. The dog trainer should have keen observation skills in order to stop testing if the animal becomes aggressive. You must feel extremely confident in your certified dog trainer's judgments and observations to avoid injury of anyone involved in the following described tests to choose an appropriate animal assisted therapy dog. Once you have chosen a competent trainer, the first task is to find a puppy or dog suitable to become an Animal Assisted Therapy dog.

Choosing an Appropriate Dog
Several authors (Burch, 2003; Granger & Kogan, 2006; and Bernard, 1995) state that the dog's health, behavior/obedience, and temperament are essential in screening potential therapy animals.

A veterinarian's responsibilities include verifying proof of vaccinations, assessment of overall health and behavior, and assessment for internal and external parasites (Bernard, 1995; Granger & Kogan, 2006). Bernard-Curran et. al, (2008) "Selecting and Choosing a Therapy Dog", adds neutering and spaying of animals.

Bernard-Curran et al. (2008) state that you should look for a dog that is calm, confident, enjoys being petted and handled, is curious, recovers from being startled, looks for human interaction, shows interest in toys, has a healthy coat, clear eyes nose, and throat, and a good appetite. Disregard dogs or puppies that show aggression, dominant traits, mouthing, excess energy, difficulty handling, extreme timidity, decreased interaction with humans, and uncertain health. Bernard-Curran et al. (2008) and Burch (2003) state that you can choose a pure breed or a mixed breed as a therapy dog. Bernard-Curran et al. (2008)

provides in-depth information regarding advantages and disadvantages of pure breeds and mixed breeds; and how to choose a good pure dog breeder. While there are good dogs in most breeds, some are more suitable than others for companionship and affection.

Luckily, I have a built-in Certified Service and Therapy dog trainer in my family, Amy Bennett, at New Hope Assistance Dogs, Inc. in Warren, PA. Amy preselected Vicki to become a service dog prior to becoming an Animal Assisted Therapy dog. By completing these tests, Amy chose Vicki when she was a puppy while observing her in her litter.

Amy Bennett (pers. com, 2008) utilized these described temperament tests that are applicable at any age; however, a puppy will need to be re-evaluated as he matures. **If at any point during testing the dog becomes even slightly aggressive, discontinue and do not consider the dog for therapy work.**

Some observable aggressive dog behaviors may include:
Biting
Barking
Scratching
Hair standing up on back
Curling lips
Showing teeth
Growling
Lunging
Snapping
Barking aggressively
Blocking your path
Showing ridge posturing
Staring
Barking
The online website http://www.k9webs.com/patscott/stresssigns.htm lists additional canine stress signs.

****

Vicki is nudging me to type something, sometimes she is so persistent. *"Oh, I remember the day in my early childhood puppy days when Amy came to visit our litter. Amy did some very interesting things. My sister Vera and I must have done some things she liked as she picked us out of all my other brothers and sisters. Here are list of some of the tests Amy completed when she choose me and my sister Vera from all our brothers and sisters."*

****

Some general tests performed by certified dog trainers in choosing an appropriate therapy dog candidate are:

1. General reaction to people: The trainer walks calmly and purposefully toward the dog then extends her hand to pet the dog. Do not kneel, use food or coax the dog. You want to see the dog's natural reaction.

>**Acceptable response:** The dog is moving into you, tail wagging, ears alert but relaxed, happy to have attention from a stranger.
>**Stop** if the dog backs away, cowers, growls, avoids contact or if he lets you touch him but he is very rigid and just tolerates it.

2. After the certified trainer greets the dog, she begins to move her hands over the dog's body. She touches his head, ears, muzzle, neck, chest, down his back, belly, paws, and tail.

>**Acceptable Response**: The dog is happy, relaxed, friendly, melting to your touching, and a little wiggly wanting more.
>**Stop** if the dog growls, puts his mouth on you, runs away, jumps at each new touch, is rigid, whips his head around and gives you a hard, cold stare.

3. Now that the certified trainer and dog are friends, she turns and walks away without coaxing the dog.

>**Acceptable behavior**: The dog will follow you, looks around then follows you, or comes to you after just talking to him. A dismissal based solely on this step should not be made; however, some red flags are having no interest in following you at all or wanting to hide and be left alone.

4. The certified trainer will coax the dog into a down position, and then gently roll him onto his back. Hold him there and make eye contact with him.

>**Acceptable behavior:** The dog rolls without a struggle, tail relaxed and behind his body; head lying on floor, looking away from eye contact (submission), and willing to remain in this position.
>**Stop** if the dog becomes very stiff or combative and refuses to roll over, rolls but keeps head lifted, tries to curl up, clamps tail tight, growls, nips, holds eye contact making you look away first.

5. The certified trainer will give the dog a treat and then place several treats on the floor. As the dog begins to eat them, pick the rest of the treats up. The trainer must use caution during this test. Once the trainer has successfully picked the food up without a reaction from the dog, she begins to give him a large treat. When it is partially in his mouth, the trainer will pull the treat back out of his mouth. Next, while the dog is eating something yummy, pet his back, head, and then his muzzle area.

Acceptable behavior: The dog's tail is wagging, unconcerned about your touch, willing to let the trainer have the treat, and relaxed.
Stop if there is any growling, snapping, and rapid gobbling of food, moving head or body to guard food.

6. Let the dog loose in the room and let him relax. While the dog is several feet away, not paying attention, drop a metal bowl on the floor. If he comes to look, praise him warmly.
> **Acceptable behavior:** The dog merely turns to look, startles slightly but recovers and comes to investigate the noise.
> **Stop** if the dog barks, bolts to other side of the room, or remains scared.

7. The trainer will start petting the dog. Then firmly give the dog a big squeeze, then firmly but gently tug his fur, ears, tail, squeeze his paws, lift his lips and feel his teeth.
> **Acceptable behavior**: The dog is happy and wagging his tail, and body relaxed; looks at you like you are crazy yet he likes it and he does not attempt to get away.
> **Stop** if there is any aggression, whipping around of the head, mouthing, pulling away, body rigidity, or refusal of touch.

8. If the trainer feels it is appropriate, arrange several people of different ages and genders to crowd around and begin petting the dog. Then have the people move closer and begin to talk loudly, arguing over who is petting the dog, etc.
> **Acceptable behavior:** The dog is wagging his tail, happy, relaxed, leaning into the peoples' touch, enjoying the attention.
> **Stop** if there is any aggression, panic, cowering, and rigid body, stiff or tucked tail and attempts to get away.

10. If the trainer feels it is appropriate, have a young child 4-6 years of age, pet the dog then abruptly yell, jump up and down, and raise his arms. Then have the child try to pet the dog again.
> **Acceptable behavior**: The dog is calm, concerned, looks at child as wondering what is wrong, and remains relaxed and happy.
> **Stop** if the dog becomes aggressive, runs away, or is skittish of the child afterwards.

11. Have the dog lie down on his side then the certified trainer will gently lie over a portion of the dog's body as if the dog were a pillow.
> **Acceptable behavior:** The dog calmly lies in place. The dog's tail is wagging there is no struggle. The dog maintains a relaxed body and is willing to remain there.
> **Stop** if the dog displays any aggression, if the dog jumps up to get away, or is stiff or unhappy.

Keep all interactions fun and positive. Give him a treat, praise him, and play with him. Let him know you are happy and that this is not punishment. Keep it brief. Your dog must enjoy this and become more tolerant of touch.

Noise is a normal part of any therapy dog's treatment environment. Amy Bennet (pers. comm., 2008) recommends you use your home environment to get your dog acclimated to unexpected noise by dropping a pan in the kitchen, or yelling to a person in the another room. When carried out in fun, your dog is rewarded with upbeat praise; and for not spooking, he will learn to trust you and accept that noise is okay.

Excitability may be an issue especially, if you are training a puppy. Amy Bennet (personal communication May 3, 2008) states you that you will need to help him learn to be calm. Do this by acting calm and soothing. Use a low voice, speak slowly, and pet him with firm but steady strokes when praising him. Your dog will learn to match your activity level and calmness.

During training times with your dog always be patient, keep it fun, give lots of love and praise, look out for the dog's safety, be consistent, and follow through with your commands.

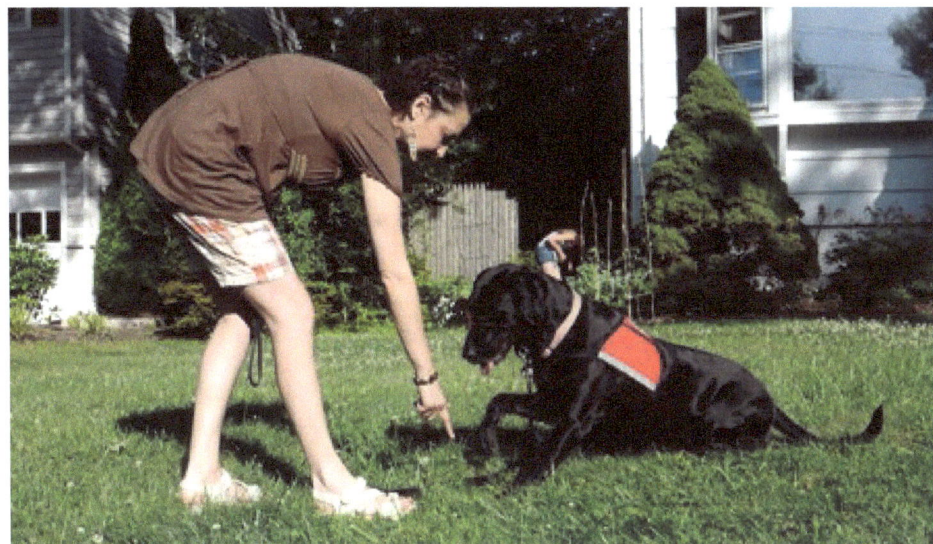

Vicki's Special Tricks

The sky is the limit! "Teach your dog to do tricks." Along with the basic obedi-ence tasks of: "sit", "down", "stay", "come" I taught Vicki commands of "up/down", "on/off", "under/over", "through" needed for obstacle courses, jumping through a hoop, "shake", catching a treat when thrown in the air, drinking from a baby bottle, picking the treat you I have in my hand with her paw, "rolling over" and "sleep". These cute tricks can really break the ice and light up a child's world. In addition, Vicki loves performing them.

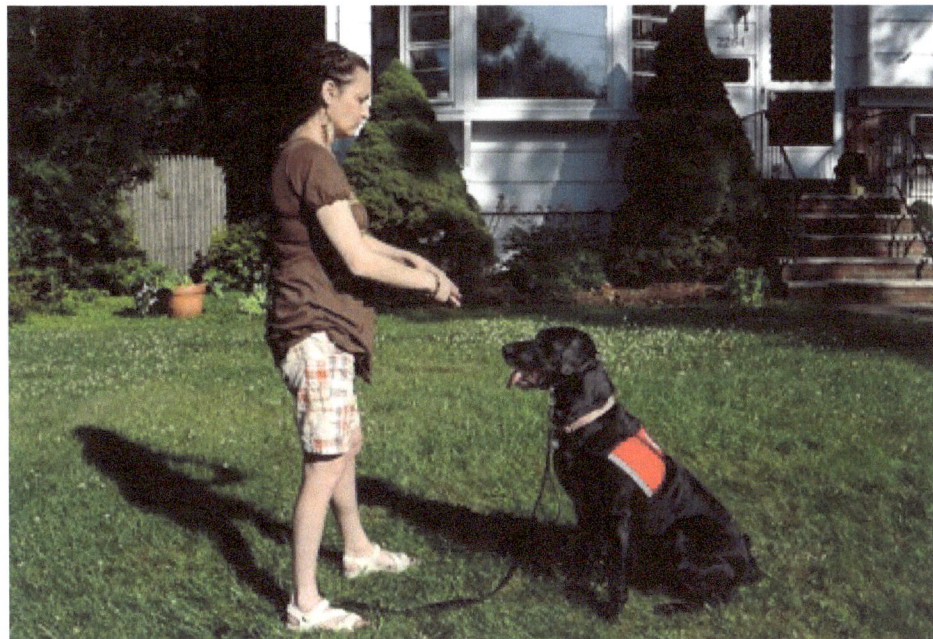

As children with ASD may not have the use of language and may be using sign language as a form of communication. I taught Vicki sign language for her commands. The child can use the word or the sign (with a little help from the handler/therapist) to follow commands. If you choose to do this type of training, these signs must be used right from the beginning of training. Vicki will follow these signs without a spoken word: "sit", "come", "down", "up", "come", "look", "wait", "sleep", and "roll over". Using signs and other creative means of communication with children with ASD is essential for communication.

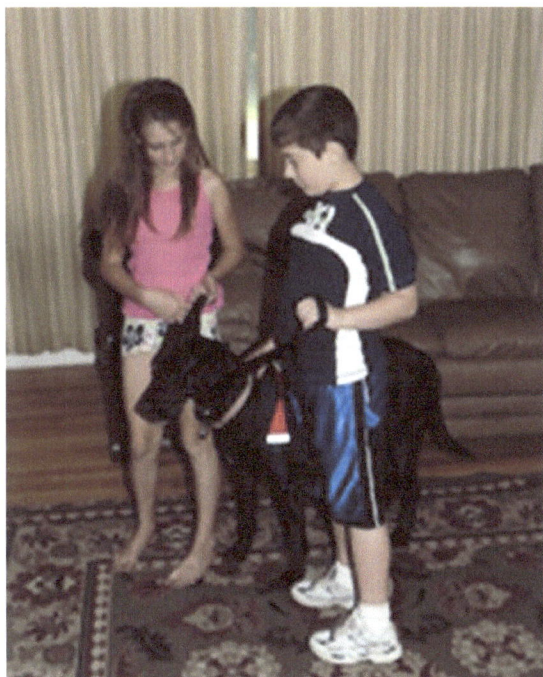

Certification
Certification exams vary depending on the reputable certified therapy program you have chosen. According to Morrison (2012), there are guidelines set up by organizations such as the Delta Society, International Association of Canine Professional, and Therapy Dogs International and the American Kennel Club Good Citizen test to determine the animal's appropriateness for AAT.

Some examples of program certifications can be found on the http://www.deltasociety.org/ (become a pet partner), www.**therapet**.com (certification steps), and www.tdi-dog.org/(testing requirements).

You may also investigate smaller organizations that certify therapy dogs. It is strongly suggested that you do your 'homework"!

Programs usually require (but are not limited too):
- Registration packet
- A team training course (extent and topics vary)
- Animal health screening with required vaccination and health record
- Pet and handlers Test
- Temperament testing
- Obedience testing
- Retesting the dog every 2-3 years.

Other programs require that you complete an AKC-Canine Good Citizen test prior to beginning the therapy dog evaluation. The AKC Canine Good Citizen certification tests, descriptions and appropriate dog behavior can be found at the website, American Kennel Club, www.akc.org.These tests include:

Test 1: Accepting a friendly stranger
Test 2: Sitting politely for petting
Test 3: Appearance and grooming
Test 4: Out for a walk (walking on a loose lead)
Test 5: Walking through a crowd
Test 6: Sit and down on command and staying in place
Test 7: Coming when called
Test 8: Reaction to another dog
Test 9: Reaction to distraction
Test 10: Supervised separation

Training collar corrective devices are usually not acceptable in testing or on visits. Some expect a gentle lead for larger dogs. Therapy dogs are usually on teams but you can just work with your dog alone, pending your selected therapy dog regulations. During testing, the dog must show **NO** signs of aggression (previously noted), jumping up, mouthing, licking, or barking.

Of course, it is important that the dog is properly trained; however, the handler must also be comfortable, competent, and have a strong relationship with the dog. The handler should have keen observation skills to constantly observe the dog's safety, behavior, and stress level cues. Fredrickson-MacNamara & Butler (2006) state the dog and handler must possess the capacity to enhance therapeutic goals and be "suitable" for the chosen population within the working environment. The handler must always respect and protect the dog's needs!

It is my belief that the handler must train the dog specifically for children on the spectrum. Besides the correct temperament, behavior, good health, and obedience, the dog must be trained for the specific autistic spectrum child population. Following sign language for hand signals, learning many obedience commands and entertaining tricks can only enhance the therapy dog team when working specifically with the pediatric autistic population.

Chapter 4: Developing a Canine Animal Assisted Therapy Program

As an occupational therapist, developing a new treatment program has always been exciting —from the beginning with writing protocols all the way through to the program's successful implementation. My new career adventure—canine animal assisted therapy—has taken me to the exhilarating "wild side" of the therapy frontier. This section is specifically written to assist both the occupational therapist interested in developing an AAT program as well as guidelines and information for parents interested in involving their autistic child in an AAT program.

Choosing a Facility
Vicki and I pursued, and successfully developed, a Canine Animal Assisted Therapy (AAT) Program in an outpatient hospital preschool program for children with autism. This program has three classes with five to eight students in each room. Vicki and I work in individual sessions, in a room or in a group classroom setting with occupational therapists, speech therapists, and special education teachers with rehabilitation aides. The chosen autistic program is based on Applied Behavioral Analysis (ABA) with the opportunity to generalize experiences in different environments. During occupational therapy and speech therapy sessions, the therapist utilizes an eclectic treatment approach.

Not being employed at this particular facility, I needed to investigate other local programs for children with autism in order to attain my goal of developing a Canine AAT program. I developed the particular program from a therapist's treatment perspective and the administrator was responsible for the necessary requirements needed for the facility. If I were an employee of the facility I may have been more active in the administrative policies, however, that decision is up to the facilities administrator and treating therapist.

At this time, there are no formal legal documentation requirements for an Animal Assisted Therapy (AAT) program. However, you must meet the requirements of your chosen facility, certified therapy canine program, and specific professional organization. Delta Society's <u>Human-Animal Health Connection,</u>

<u>Animal Assisted Therapy, Standards of Practice</u> (1996) provides an extensive checklist guide to Standards of Practice, along with additional appendices of invaluable information on Facility Assessment, AAT Providers, Provider Organizations, Service Delivery, Animals, and Investigative Studies. This book provides detailed and specific criteria questions you can use throughout the canine AAT program development process.

As a therapist, you may already have a facility at which you would like to develop an AAT Program for children on the autistic spectrum. However, if you do not yet have a facility in mind, start by investigating public school systems, inpatient and outpatient private school systems, or specialized children's rehabilitation facilities.

Begin by calling your chosen facility and telling them you are interested in discussing a Canine AAT program. This initial step will move you to the next level if an administrator will discuss the possibility of establishing a program.

When you find that an administrator or decision maker is interested in the AAT program, set up a meeting time to tour the facility and discuss its programs. When you meet with the administrator, thoroughly explain that you would like to work with them in setting up a Canine AAT program to help children on the autistic spectrum. You can use the presentation (Appendix A) or the handout to presentation (Appendix B) as a guideline for your initial meeting or conversation.

In this discussion, be certain to include and describe possible AAT goals and ways that a therapist may be able to achieve them. For example, the occupational therapist conducts the therapy session using the dog as a modality to facilitate independent functioning in the areas of self-help, play, and learning. A further example may be the child increasing hand skills by opening different containers to feed the dog treats and fasten or to unfasten the dog's vest or collar.

Remember, although they are interviewing you, you are also interviewing them to see if you want to pursue a canine AAT program with their particular facility. Therefore, do not hesitate to ask as many questions as you feel necessary in reaching your decision.

<u>Here are some additional questions you may want to ask:</u>
- How many children are in your program?
- What are the children's ages?
- What treatment methods do you use in your program (ABA, Greenspan, The Miller Method, Sensory Integration, other)?
- Do you feel your staff would be interested in an AAT program?
- Can you appoint a coordinator or act as the AAT program liaison?
- Can we set up a time when I may conduct a presentation to your staff, with the dog present?
- Is there an appropriate room available to conduct individual or group sessions?
- Would you like to meet the dog?

- What administrative policies must you have to begin a canine assisted therapy program?

Discuss consent forms, policy and procedures, risk management, liability, infection control, payment (if applicable), staff and training requirements, volunteer training, parental consent forms, and professional documentation requirements. The Delta Society, www.deltasociety.org, recommends viewing the following video with the facility prior to starting an AAT program: *Introducing Visiting Animal Programs*.

Assuming that the conversation or interview goes well, follow up with a Thank You letter. Provided is an example of a Thank You letter as if you were going to pursue this facility (please refer to Appendix C). In the last sentence of the letter, provide possible dates to meet and discuss further details of the Canine AAT program.

Choosing a Canine AAT Team

The other scenario is that you already have a facility wanting to start an animal assisted therapy program. Where do they begin?

Forming a great match between facility and professional rehabilitation dog handler makes a significant impact on whether the Canine AAT Program will be a success. It is ideal if an autistic rehabilitation specialist on the treatment team is chosen as the certified dog handler, as she is trained to clinically reason in treatment sessions to maximize the child's treatment outcomes. However, there are more volunteer certified dog handlers available that can be assets to your program if properly educated, constantly evaluated and clinically guided by rehabilitation professional. You can find a certified dog teams on The Delta Society website, www.deltasociety.org, Therapy Dog International website: www.tdi-dog.org, searching additional websites for local facilities, or by asking a veterinarian. I would suggest you further investigate the program prior to making our decision.

Once you have chosen a program and have a volunteer lined up to interview, have the Canine AAT program director and program coordinator/liaison interview the volunteer and her dog.

Some suggested questions:
- Is your dog a certified therapy dog?
- Where was the therapy dog certified (more specifically, at what facility)?
- Have you successfully completed an obedience class?
- Does your dog have up-to-date vaccinations and regular check ups with your veterinarian?
- Can you provide documentation for certification, obedience training, and vaccination certification?

- How long have you and your dog been certified as a team?
- Have you provided AAA or AAT services? Do you have references that I can contact?
- Do you have experience with the autistic population?
- What got you interested in forming a certified dog team?
- Why would you like to work with this particular population?

You may want to have someone available to observe how the team interacts with a stranger and in a new environment. This interview gives you the opportunity to observe the dog and handler in action. You can observe important aspects such as the dog's cleanliness and temperament, and interaction between dog and handler.

Educating Staff

Whether you are an administrator, volunteer with the certified therapy program coordinator, or a rehabilitation team member for those on the autistic spectrum starting a program, education is essential. The facility must educate all practitioners involved in the treatment program.

During the scheduled meeting with the liaison and administrator, discuss and arrange a staff educational in-service time and decide who is most qualified to present the information. Discuss and provide the Lecture to Facility Staff (Appendix A), Canine Animal Assisted Therapy Presentation Handout (Appendix B), Individual Treatment Session Protocol (Appendix D), Group Treatment Session Protocol (Appendix E), Responsibilities of the Therapist and the Dog Handler (Appendix F), Client Referral Form (Appendix G) and Therapy Sign Up Sheet (Appendix H).

If necessary, review and change the forms to meet the facility's needs. In the meeting, decide and ask the liaison to photocopy what handouts you would like to provide the staff at the in-service presentation. I have provided Appendix B, Appendix D, Appendix E, Appendix F, Appendix G, and Appendix H.

It is also essential to educate the parents about the Canine Animal Assisted Therapy Program. The program coordinator or administrator may set this up. I had a wonderful opportunity to educate the children's parents with Vicki present. During this parental educational experience, set up by the program liaison, I used a modified version of the staff in-service and handout. At the end of the in-service, with parental consent, children were able to join us to meet Vicki. Thankfully, the children's responses were all favorable and the parents were excited. We were able to complete a group activity and some children stayed after for a one to one experience. Fun was had by all!

Education of staff and parents is an important aspect of any program's development. It is essential that all individuals involved in developing the program be present, at the educational in-service (especially the administrator and liaison) to answer questions regarding hospital administration and facility issues. An informational, fun-filled and enthusiastic presentation provides excitement and energy to get the program started. Luckily, I had the fantastic experience of having the entire team of rehabilitation professionals present.

Liability Insurance
The dog handler should investigate liability insurance, beginning by investigating whether or not the facility or the dog certification program covers your liability. If not, the certification program may be able to assist you in getting the coverage. Pichot & Coulter (2007) also suggest examining the handler's professional liability policy, home insurance policy, and an umbrella insurance policy through your personal insurance company. Wherever you obtain your liability insurance, it is essential to have a copy in writing for our own files.

Documentation
Client documentation should be addressed to all rehabilitation members to meet the requirement of the facility and for reimbursement. The Delta Society Standards of Practice (1996) suggest that the treating therapist utilizing the therapy dog document long term and short term goals only under their scope of clinical practice; re-evaluate, modify and adopt interventions and goals as appropriate; and identify ways to measure treatment progress. Pichot & Coulter (2007) provide an Individual Treatment Plan specifically related to counseling; however, it can be modified and utilized for an autistic rehabilitation team if the therapists and the administrators like this type of format. I have developed a method to establish goals and collect data in Appendix G. The documentation format that is utilized must meet the requirements and reimbursement criteria of the chosen facility.

Recommended Facility Requirements
It is necessary that the facility administrator meet all the facility requirements needed for the Canine AAT program. This may include, but is not limited to, policy and procedures, risk management, liability issues, infection control, payment if applicable, staff training requirements, volunteer training, parental consent forms, and professional documentation requirements. Bernard (1995) and Pichot & Coulter (2007) provide samples of Animal Assisted Therapy Policies and Procedures.

It would be beneficial for the administrator to involve the program liaison, the dog handler (volunteer or therapist), health care professionals and special education teachers, in the facility-documented requirements. As all involved in the program may have different views and concerns that, perhaps the administrator has not thought about addressing.

Children Not Appropriate for AAT

The Delta Society website http://www.deltasociety.org/ AnimalsAAAAbout.htm#notbeneficial, states that AAT programs are not beneficial for people who are fearful and/or aggressive, have allergies or a compromised immune system, possess a concern with family or cultural views of animals, and susceptible to zoonotic diseases (this is when a dog can transmit diseases to a human). The Delta Society website includes a list of many other individuals who may not benefit from an AAT program; however, I felt these aforementioned concerns were necessary to note regarding the population of children on the autistic spectrum.

For good safety practices, general precautions are crucial in preventing zoonotic diseases. The following safety precautions are complied from The Center for Disease Control (www.cdc.gov/) and Companion Animal Parasite control (www.capcvet.org.)

Zoonotic Prevention and Precautions

During and after all therapy sessions:
- Supervise children to make sure they wash their hands well with running water and soap after touching the dog.
- Do not let the child put his hands or other object in his mouth after touching dog.
- Never allow anyone to touch a dog's stool.
- Do not allow the dog to lick anyone.
- Do not allow anyone to kiss the dog.

Handler's safety precautions:
- Practice good hygiene by washing hands with soap and running water.
- Do not allow your dog to eat undercooked or raw meat.
- Do not allow your dog to eat from a garbage can or drink from the toilet.
- Do not allow your dog near other animals' stool.
- Do not allow your dog to hunt, or prey upon, other animals.
- Take your dog to the veterinarian to check for infections if he has diarrhea for 1-2 days.
- Do not take your dog to therapy sessions if she is sick.
- Have your dog tested for parasites at least once a year.
- Administer preventative and year-round worming, flea and tick medications.
- Have your dog well bathed and groomed with nails trimmed.
- Avoid high traffic pet areas (for example, dog parks).
- Clean up all dog stools daily.
- Attend all veterinarian appointments for physical examinations and testing.
- Ask your veterinarian any additional questions about parasite infection risks and preventative measures.

Following the earlier mentioned guidelines, the rehabilitation team should then decide which children are appropriate for Canine AAT. The liaison, dog handler, and the facilities administration, should plan on how they shall introduce the dog to the children. Safety should be everyone's first and utmost priority. For example, we decided to bring a child, special education teacher, certified therapy dog and dog handler into a room for the first introduction. The special education teacher and the dog handler closely observed the child and dog. The child approached the dog on his own terms. If the child responded positively and safely to the dog, the child was placed into the canine AAT program.

Group and Individual Treatment Options
The Canine Animal Assisted Program offers many treatment options. Treatment options include: one or two children in a theme based activity, an individual Special Education, Occupational Therapy, Speech Therapy session, a chosen two to three child group session, or a classroom group session. Individual or two-three group treatment sessions are usually fifteen-minute sessions, and classroom treatment session times range from a half hour to one hour. Regardless of the treatment options, the rehabilitation professional's clinical reasoning skills are needed to facilitate the child's maximum functional abilities.

Initially, in this facility, the special education teachers took the lead in identifying children appropriate for the program. The special education teachers established individualized treatment goals and therapy sheets to monitor progress. Appendix G provides a professional team referral form.

Due to the overwhelming response to the program, we began the fifteen-minute sessions with one or two children focusing on a particular task theme. For example, "A Picnic with Vicki" theme: the child or children and special education teacher set up the picnic area blanket, paper dishes and cups, then fake plastic food was set on each plate. The handler distributed treats, via plate or in the child's hand, to feed Vicki and baby bottle to have Vicki drink. The child and the teacher had the opportunity provide food and a drink to Vicki.

As the program continued with additional aforementioned activities, treatment options evolved. Seeking out and educating occupational therapists and speech therapists were other keys to the program's success. When the therapists observed the children's positive responses and incorporation of the dog into treatment, I believed they realized they had another modality they could use to reach the children on the spectrum. Vicki and I soon began doing some individual therapy sessions.

Vicki and I were becoming a very brave team, motivated and inspired to handle a larger group of children. We "decided" to suggest beginning a classroom group session. This required a great relationship with the classroom teacher, communication, and coordination of treatment activities.

Several days prior to the scheduled canine animal assisted therapy time, I contacted the special education teachers via email. The teachers decided which children would be seen and in what treatment context. I usually suggested a treatment theme, group activities, and some individual treatment ideas. I tried to incorporate the child's applied behavioral analysis task, the alphabet letter person, or any tasks currently being taught in the classroom and e-mailed my suggestions back to the special education teacher. When we decided on the activities, the special education teacher and I brought necessary supplies for the treatment session. Luckily, I have my own "treasure chest" of supplies and toys and the treatment center has a wealth of state-of-the-art equipment.

Ideally, I would suggest that canine animal assisted therapy last about one hour, one session a week. However, the treatment time is negotiable throughout the program. It is crucial to remember that it is the responsibility of the handler to know your certified therapy dog well and look out for any signs of canine stress. You always want the dog to enjoy his visits with the children. My hope and goal is that when Vicki and I leave all of our sessions, we have been a wonderful experience for everyone involved.

Once all the required necessary information is in place, I have provided the required treating therapist forms needed (Appendixes A-H, my resume, Vicki's dog obedience training certificate, therapy dog certification and vaccination record, and suggested reading articles) in a binder for the facility. I recommend that the facility add whatever specific requirements to the binder.

I have had a fantastic experience developing this Canine AAT program. I hope I have provided you the information and tools needed for the same success.

Chapter 5: Integrating Your Certified Animal Assisted Therapy Dog Into the Autism Spectrum Disorder Rehabilitation Team

The Autism Spectrum Disorder (ASD) treatment methods are abundant and can be overwhelming. The four more extensive treatment methods chosen, The *Floor Time Approach (DIR), Sensory Integration (SI), The Miller Method and Applied Behavior Analysis (ABA),* will be briefly discussed as each treatment method is well beyond the scope of this book. Therapists providing these treatments require specialized training; therefore, possible Canine Animal Assisted Therapy activities are provided to facilitate the reader's clinical reasoning skills to integrate appropriate activities into these chosen treatment methods.

The DIR (Developmental, Individual-Difference, Relationship-Based)/The Floor Time Approach
This developmental approach to autism treatment developed by Stanley Greenspan is based on interactive play that is both fun and spontaneous. Greenspan, Wieder, & Simon (1998), state that in the Floor Time Approach the therapists, caregivers, educators, and parents assist the child in mastering fundamental development skills or milestones. Each previous milestone must be mastered prior to building on the next developmental milestone.

<u>Developmental Milestones</u> (Greenspan, DeGangi, & Wieder, 2001)
>**Developmental stage 1: 0-3 months** referred to as *Self-Regulation and Interest in the World.* During this milestone, the child has a dual ability to take interest in the sights, sounds and sensations of the world and calm oneself down.
>**Developmental Stage 2: 2-7 months** referred to as *Intimacy.* During this milestone, the child has the ability to engage in relationships with other people, primarily parents and caregivers.

Developmental Stage 3: 3-10 months referred to as *Two Way Communication*. During this milestone, the child responds to gestures and initiates social interactions. Two-way communication is essential for all human interaction, so the child can see the world in a logical manner.

Developmental Stage 4: 9-18 months referred to as *Complex Communication* (Complex Sense of Self). During this milestone, the child has the ability to string together a series of actions and gestures to communicate fairly complex thoughts. The child expresses himself with creativeness and uses gestures as a prerequisite to speech.

Developmental Stage 5: 18-30 months referred to as *Emotional Ideas*. During this milestone, the child uses play to formulate ideas. The child can use gestures and pictures, and then begins to use words to communicate his needs. As the child increases the use of his vocabulary, he begins to understand that symbols stand for things; hence increasing his interaction in pretend play.

Developmental Stage 6: 30-48 months referred to as *Emotional Thinking*. During this milestone, through play the child builds bridges between ideas to make them reality based and logical. The child now verbalizes more often in expressing his ideas and feelings.

Depending on the severity of the child's autistic spectrum disorder, the trained professional must closely observe the child to grade the activity in meeting the child's developmental milestone. Greenspan, Wieder, & Simon (1998) provide the professional with treatment strategies to facilitate the child's progression through the developmental milestones. Some of these treatment strategies are: opening circles of communication (elaborating on whatever interests the child at that moment); following the child's lead (being a supportive play partner, letting the child set the pace and direction of play); extending and expanding play (asking questions, keeping the creative play drama going); and closing the circles of communication (the therapist will use comments, statements or gestures in play, and the child will close the line of communication with his own statements and gestures). These circles of communication continue in succession as the child continues to understand and benefit from the importance of two-way communication.

In the Floor Time Approach, a dog can readily serve as a facilitator for communication. By following the child's lead with the dog, you can use several activities. The child can initiate petting the dog while someone else asks questions about the dog. For example, "where are the dog's ears?" This initiated topic can facilitate further communication by asking the child to point to his ears, then point to the therapist's ears. Other initiated topics are: "How many paws does a dog have?" "What other animals have four paws? and "What color is the dog?"

Other activities may include the therapist placing dog treats in many types of plastic jars and giving them to the child to open. Some of the jars can be screwed tightly shut, encouraging the child to initiate asking for help in getting the treat to feed the dog. Another activity can be playing Peek-a-Boo with the therapist and dog to facilitate the child's social interactions. Additional treatment suggestions are in Chapter Six under " themed activities." The website http://www.coping.org/intervention/floortm.htmn, provides a comprehensive overview of The Floor Time Approach.

Sensory Integration Developed by Jean Ayres
Ayres' (2000) definition of Sensory Integration is "The organization of sensory input for use. The 'use' may be a perception of the body or world, or an adaptive response, or learning process, or the development of some neural function. Through sensory integration, many parts of the nervous system work together so that a person can interact with the environment effectively and experience satisfaction."

Sensory Integration has extensive theory and a multitude of treatment techniques. Sensory Integration is the ability to receive and interpret sensory information from the environment and demonstrate adaptive or appropriate responses. This sensory information comes from the classic "five senses" touch, taste, smell, sound, and visual stimuli, in addition to proprioceptive input (which tells us which position our body is in, and how to grade movements), and vestibular input (which tells us where our body is in space, and gives us a sense of balance). Children with autism usually display hypersensitivity or hyposensitivity to sensory input which interferes with their ability to function in everyday life skills.

An example of a child with Sensory Integration Dysfunction might be displaying hypersensitivity to touch and not liking to have his face washed, hair combed, walking barefoot, touching certain textures, or feeling uncomfortable with seams or clothing tags. If the child is hyposensitive to proprioceptive sensation, he may flap hands, lean into people or objects, or crash into objects. Ayres (2000) shows, in a chart form, ineffectively functioning sensory systems leading to difficulties with motor planning, bilateral coordination, body awareness, attention span, organization, self-esteem, visual perception, and learning.

In the Sensory Integration Approach, the therapist must be well aware of the child's sensory preferences and thus choose appropriate activities. The animal assisted therapy dog can be a phenomenal facilitator in meeting sensory needs. The therapist can utilize petting, grooming, brushing, washing and hugging the dog to increase the child's ability to tolerate touch or different textures. The therapist can lead the dog or follow the child through an obstacle course or playground equipment, can walk with dog through cones, or pull the dog in a wagon to provide the child with vestibular and proprioceptive input. Additional activities can be found in Chapter Six under "Sensory Needs."

The Miller Method: A Cognitive-Developmental Systems Approach (2007)
The Miller Method was developed by Arnold and Eileen Eller-Miller. The Millers, with Chretien (2007) believe that typical development depends on the ability to form systems. Systems, also defined as organized chunks of behavior, perception or thought, are initially repeated then expanded as the child develops. Miller identifies and addresses issues of body, social, communication, and symbolic systems. Children on the autistic spectrum display faulty systems that stall their early developmental progression; distorting and inhibiting advanced developmental stages.

The treatment strategies used to assist the child in transforming his disordered behavior into functional activity are best described by Miller himself. Miller, on his website (http://www.millermethod.org) describes major treatment strategies to restore normal development progressions: "One involves the transformation of children's aberrant systems (lining up blocks, driven reactions to stimuli, etc.) into functional behaviors; the other is the systematic and repetitive introduction of developmentally relevant activities involving objects and people. Activities are chosen to fill developmental gaps. ." This process is facilitated by narrating the children's actions while they are elevated 2.5 feet above the ground on an Elevated Square and similar challenging structures. Elevating the children enhances sign-word guidance of behavior and body-other awareness as well as motor-planning and social-emotional contact. It also helps children transition from one engaging object or event to another or from object involvement to representational play."

In the Miller Method, the dog can be a facilitator next to, or on, the elevated square as a change in the system. For example, each station of the square helps the child expand his play. At the first station, the child can pick up the brush and brush his hair; at the second station the child can brush his mom's hair; at the third station he can pick up the brush and the brush the dog; and at the last station, brush a stuffed dog.

During this activity, the child can use a picture exchange communication system (PECS), sign language, or the spoken word to improve his ability to communicate. The dog can lead or follow the child on the set up elevated square.

Another activity is expanding the child's play off of the elevated square. Once the child has mastered pouring water out of bottles, he can pour water for the dog to drink. Expanding this activity further can be pouring dog food into a bowl to feed the dog.

Applied Behavioral Analysis (ABA) is based on behavioral theory and expanded upon by Ivar Lovaas. Anderson (2007) simply states that ABA is "the use of the scientific principles of behavior to form, maintain and decrease desired behaviors and to diminish less desirable behaviors. This can involve a number of different strategies and can be used across a wide variety of situations and people in order to change/teach behavior."

Buchanan & Weiss (2006) state that tasks are broken down into their simplest elements in an intensive, structured teaching program. The child is presented with a stimulus through discrete trials. These discrete trials consist of three parts: (1) the request or instruction (stimulus) (2) the child's response (response to stimulus) and (3) response feedback (consequence). Correct responses get rewarded and incorrect responses get ignored or negatively rewarded.

Green (1997-2008) http://www.behavior.org/autism/ states that effective ABA treatment programs combine discrete trials with other ABA methods (incidental teaching procedures, chaining, etc.) in generalizing trained skills to everyday situations with importance placed on positive social interactions and making learning enjoyable. Buchanan & Weiss (2006) document several ABA treatment techniques in their book Applied Behavior Analysis and Autism.

For example, the antecedent could be "touch nose;," the desired behavior is the child touching his nose, and the consequence (positive or negative reinforcement) could be saying "Great!" or offering something that the child is motivated to work for (a toy, a particular food, etc). If he does not touch his nose, the reinforcement may be saying "Let's try again!" or "No." At any time, the trainer may use prompts to assist the child in being aware of what the practitioner expects of him. Perhaps she would place her hand on the child's hand and guide it towards his nose, or she may use a verbal or visual cue. Extensive data based on the trainer's observations is employed to determine when each skill is mastered. This determines the next goal in teaching a skill or the maintenance of a behavior.

One of the biggest criticisms in the ABA method is the child becomes "robotic" only performing the tasks given in discrete trials when the provider states the command in a continual repetitive way. The dog can be utilized as a transitional object to assist the child to begin to interact with the outside world beyond discrete trials.

When using animal assistive therapy in ABA treatment, the dog can assist the child in generalizing a task to a different setting. Using the example of touching your own nose, the child can touch his nose, the therapist's nose, and then the dog's nose. This task can be repeated with additional body parts. Other activities that can be integrated into the ABA method are functional activities of self-care listed in Chapter Six.

The therapist or special education teacher can use creativity to integrate the therapy dog into the treatment session for autism spectrum disorder. Whatever the chosen method of treatment, the possibilities are limitless!

Chapter 6:
Canine Therapeutic Activities

This practical chapter provides individual and group goals and treatment suggestions you can utilize during AAT.

INDIVIDUAL TREATMENT GOALS AND ACTIVITIES
Physical

Improve hand and fine motor skills:
⇒ Have the child manipulate buckles on therapy dog's vest, clasps on leashes, and collars.
⇒ Make a special vest with clothes fasteners on it.
⇒ Place small pieces of treats in egg carton holes to improve pincer skills.
⇒ Have the child open plastic eggs, Ziploc containers, bags, peanut butter jars, and small bottles filled with small of treats and feed treats to dog.
⇒ Draw and color dog.
⇒ Use dog paw stamps, cut out paws, dog stickers, outline the dog to make to play pin the tail on the dog, dog crafts.
⇒ Write about the dog.
⇒ String wooden animals with lace.
⇒ Dot to dot dog worksheets.
⇒ Breaking up dog treats into small pieces.

Improve gross motor skills:
⇒ Have the child follow the dog through a simple obstacle course.
⇒ Kick and throw a ball and have the dog can retrieve it.
⇒ Crawl like a dog.
⇒ Have a small dog stand on a raised table and ask the child to stand while stroking or brushing the animal's back and head. This activity can be modified by proper placement of the dog.
⇒ Position the dog to reach in various directions, challenging balance.
⇒ Walk the dog for short distances on different surfaces and inclines around the facility. (The handler should use a double lead and walk alongside the dog and child).
⇒ Ambulate around cones or other desired obstacles.

⇒ Go onto playground equipment with the child.
⇒ Song "Doggie" and "The Doggie Went Over the Mountain"
⇒ Build a large doghouse using therapy equipment, a bed sheet and clothes pins.

Language

Improve ability to communicate:

⇒ Discuss the features of the dog – for example color of dog, how many legs a dog has, fur texture, ears - and expand on this conversation: What other animals have four legs? Can you name some other colors?
⇒ Write a story about the dog.
⇒ Tell a story about the dog.
⇒ Introduce yourself and the dog and tell a fact about the dog.
⇒ Read a story to the dog.
⇒ Have the dog follow simple commands by using sign language or speech (come, sit, stay, stop, up, and look).
⇒ Ask the child what a happy, sad, tired, or angry dog looks like (the handler would lift dog's lip). The child can imitate the way the dog would look as the handler gets the animal to perform the suggested emotion. The therapist can then ask the child to perform a person's specific emotion.
⇒ Incorporate any sign language into session. Sign for "drink" and then have the child give a drink to the dog.
⇒ Increase vocabulary: Facilitate sounds and words during sessions.

⇒ Use the Picture Exchange Communication System (PECS) with dog treats, colors, or a dog sitting.

⇒ Give the child a choice of two objects. For example, show the child a ball and a dog brush, then have child point to or verbalize his choice.

Cognitive/Educational

Increase attention to task:

⇒ Attention to task is constantly monitored via minutes or seconds.

Increase the ability to follow simple directions:

⇒ Follow one and two-step commands - get treat from the bag and feed it to the dog, get brush from bag and brush the dog, get the treat out of the dog's vest and give it to her.

⇒ Follow commands (word and sign language) that the dog can follow.

Increase eye contact:

⇒ Eye contact can be improved upon by placing treats near the therapist's face, or placing treats behind the therapist's back to facilitate communication.

Increase ability to point to, and identify, body parts:

⇒ Point to dog's body part, then have the child point to his own similar body part, and then to the therapist's similar body part.

⇒ Mr. Potato Head – The therapist can ask the child to point to the dog's body part then his own body part, and then place the appropriate body part on Mr. Potato Head.

Increase directionality (on /off, up/ down, over/under, in/out.):

⇒ Directionality is incorporated by using blankets or obstacles.

Improve knowledge of colors:

⇒ Ask the dog's color, and then expand conversation by asking names of similar colored objects.

Sensory Needs

Improve the child's ability to tolerate tactile stimulation (petting, touching, brushing, washing) for a specific time period:

⇒ Touch, pet, and brush the dog.

⇒ Place several textures on the back of the brush.

⇒ Squeeze sponges, lather, and rinse while washing the dog.

⇒ Slowly, and rhythmically, pet the dog.

⇒ Touch different textures on the dog: ears, back, paws, and belly.

Provide proprioceptive stimuli to improve the child's attention to task and organizational skills:

⇒ Lean, hug, or cuddle with the dog.

⇒ Carry, push or pull dog or dog toys to proper treatment area.

⇒ Devise obstacle courses.

⇒ March and jog slowly with dog.

Provide vestibular input to improve the child's attention span:

⇒ Have the dog dance or spin in a circle, and then the child imitates

the dog.
⇒ Dance the "Hokey Pokey."
⇒ Sing and gesture "Head, Shoulders, Knees and Toes."
⇒ Have the dog roll over or down an inclined mat, then the child imitates the dog.

ADLs (Activities of Daily Living)

Improve self-care (feeding, grooming, dressing, etc) to age appropriate level:

Feeding Skills:

⇒ Give the dog a drink from his bowl, and then the child takes a drink from his cup.

⇒ Give the dog a drink from his bottle, and then the child takes a drink from his bottle.

Grooming Skills:
⇒ Brush the dog with dog brush and then child will brush his hair with his own brush.
⇒ Wash the dog's face with washcloth then the child will wash his face with his own washcloth.
⇒ Wash the dog's paws, and then wash your hands.

Dressing Skills:
⇒ Play Dress-up: Have the child place a hat on the dog and then child can place his own hat on himself. Continue tasks with other clothing items.

GROUP TREATMENT GOALS:

To increase socialization skills:
Increase verbal interactions between children
Increase participation in a group setting
Improve interactions with teachers
Improve interactions with dog and dog handler
Increase awareness of others

To improve pretend play/imaginative play:
Increase cognitive flexibility ability to tolerate three small changes in pretend play activity with dog.
Increase ability to engage in pretend play activity for two minutes with another child and dog.

THEME ACTIVITIES:
Games: Play <u>Twister</u> with dog sitting on color, trace dog and make tails.
Then, play "pin the tail on the dog"; or "hide and seek" where the dog and
handler hide and the child finds the dog; or "follow the leader."

Songs: Sing "Head, Shoulders, Knees, and Toes" with the child pointing to his own body parts then to the dog's body parts or the Hokey Pokey.

Construct obstacle courses:
Have a picnic, with the child and therapist setting out the tablecloth, animal plates, cups and napkins, and pretend food; and feeding the dog treats and drinks.

Play "Doctor": Have the child check the dogs' and therapists' ears, nose, heart, and other body parts.

Play Dress-up: Dress up the dog in a hat, scarf, necklace, socks, shoes, skirt or top, and then have the child dress himself up. Have the child dress in a dog costume and act like the dog when he is sleeping, happy, or mad.

Have a "dog grooming day" (washing, and brushing dog).
Host a "dog birthday party."

Set up a miniature store using play money and dog items. Have the handler and dog come in to the store ask for a dog treat, exchange the money, and then receive the products.

Play "veterinarian" with a medical kit.

GROUP CLASSROOM ACTIVITIES
Color and Treat: This game can incorporate identifying colors, fine motor skills, socialization skills, turn taking, and signing.

One child passes out colored cups, while another child can pass out treats to place in the cups. The therapist calls out or signs a specifically colored cup, then the child with that color cup approaches the dog and feeds him his treat.

Dog March: This activity can incorporate goals related to sensorimotor skills, attention, following directions, signing, and motor planning.

All the children form a circle with the therapists, dog and handler. You may want to start with the children walking in a circle, stomping their feet, or marching. Use spoken language or signing to communicate "stop" (everyone stops in place), then communicate, "go" and the children begin to move in a circle again. Other commands can be incorporated that the dog can follow with the children such as "sit", "up", "down", and "sleep".

Dress-up Game:

Place children's clothing into one bag then place dog's clothing into another bag. Play music, and then stop the music. Whatever child the music stops on, have him reach into the dog's bag and choose a piece of clothing to dress the dog. Then have him reach into the children's bag and choose a piece of clothing the child will dress in.

Tactile Game:

Obtain cotton balls, light sand papers, wooden blocks, and wet napkins. Give each child one of the obtained items such as a cotton ball. Ask or sign "what does the cotton ball feel like? (answer: soft) and then ask "what part of the dog feels that same way? (answer: ears, fur).

In group treatments, I like to start with a sensorimotor activity, then proceed with a cognitive/educational task, and finish with a craft activity. Listed below are previously utilized, successful group treatment sessions.

(Every session begins with an introduction and interaction with the dog.)

Classroom Group Session Example 1

1.   The children, teachers, dog and dog handler march while following commands. We have used the commands of "sit", "down", "stay", "sleep", "roll over", "happy dog", "sleepy dog", "sad dog", and "angry dog (I will hold up Vicki's teeth to demonstrate).

2.   Each child chooses a string animal. If the animal has four legs like Vicki, child places animal on the string.

3.   The dog handler gets the dog to wag its tail. The children imitate the dog's movement and then state what emotion they think the dog is expressing; for example happy, sad, or angry.

4.   The child draws and colors the dog in one of the displayed emotions (i.e. happy, play dog), then draws his face with that same emotion.

Classroom Group Session Example 2

1. The dog and child complete a simple obstacle course of one to three tasks.

2. Each child, taking turns, is asked to point to a specific body part on himself, then on the dog's body (i.e. nose, head, ears,).

3. Lastly, using a coloring picture of a dog, the therapist directs the child to color the dog's nose green, the dogs' paws blue, etc.

Classroom Group Session Example 3

1. The group performs sensorimotor movement songs, such as the "Hokey Pokey" and "Head, shoulders, knees and toes," with a rotating child assistant helping with the dog.

2. Each child has his own hat, shoes, socks and some dress up clothes. One of the children helps the dog handler put a specific clothes item on dog, then each child places that same clothing item on himself.

3. Lastly, each child draws a picture of the dog with clothes on.

Classroom Group Session Example 4

1. An obstacle course is arranged to teach opposites (i.e., up/down, over under). Each child follows the dog, one at a time, on the obstacle course telling the therapist what movement he will perform before he starts.

For example, we have used plastic stairs to facilitate a child in communicating "up and down", a solid plastic foam square for "on and off", a mat placed in a tent form for "in and out", and a bolster with something supporting it on both sides for "under and over".

2. Each child will have an opportunity to give a command to dog in the most effective way he is learning to communicate. Once the dog completes the command, he will give her praise by petting her and giving her a treat.

3. Finally, we have used play dough to construct dogs, or made dog faces.

Many activities will depend on the developmental level of the child and the skill level of the dog. You can always "teach your dog new tricks!"

Classroom Group Session Example 5

1. Have dog lie down on side, on poster boards. Each child gets a chance to outline a part of the dog.

2. Have the children make and cut out tails from construction paper.

3. Tape a pre made dog outline on the wall. If tolerated, spin child with blindfold on and have him place the tale the poster board dog. Meanwhile the dog and the children are watching and interacting.

4. Then each child can take a turn putting the rest of the features on the dog (nose, mouth, etc).

These goals and activities are derived from the following sources:
Renee Jensen, Occupational Therapist. Author of the book.

Gammonley et al. (1997) Delta Society: The Human-Animal Health Connection Animal-Assisted Therapy.
The Activity Idea Place: An Early Childhood Educator's Resource. http://www.123child.com/act/

The most exciting part of occupational therapy treatment has been exploring fun-filled children's activities; in this case, with the additional challenge of integrating a therapy dog. Vicki and I had the opportunity to try most of them with great success. We hope you have the same experience!

CHAPTER 7: Conclusion

Autistic Spectrum Disorder continues to be on the rise in the United States. Although strides have been made, the etiology of Autism remains a mystery. Although there are extensive autistic spectrum disorder treatment theories and treatment techniques, therapists are "thinking outside the box" to find additional ways to help children with autism.

For centuries, animals have been companions to humans. Since the 1960's animal assisted therapy has become increasing popular, bringing about extensive research studies, books and articles on Animal Assisted Activity (AAA) and Animal Assisted Therapy (AAT). Therapy dog organizations specifically began to differentiate between AAA and AAT; providing a plethora of information on benefits, development of programs, policies and procedures, and risk management.

The guidance of such organizations was needed to help others begin a wonderful journey towards a therapy dog team to help autistic children; however, specific additional information was needed to assist the reader and/or dog handler to work specifically with these children. I believe the volunteer/handler must have an extensive knowledge in working with autistic children. This knowledge is necessary to meet the child's needs and to train the dog properly to work with this population. It would be ideal if a therapist on the rehabilitation team were the dog handler, because he would have professional knowledge base and clinical reasoning skills, for the facilities specific therapy base, trained in guiding the treatment and look for of specific child's behavior.

Whether a volunteer and a dog, or a therapist and dog become the therapy dog team a specific AAT Program is essential. AAT program development involves many of hours of time and patience. For an AAT program to be implemented, the volunteer or therapist, certified dog program coordinator, facility administrator and liaison must have an excellent rapport. One of the most important skills of the volunteer or therapist pursuing an AAT program is excellent communication skills. This is crucial to be able to clearly and concisely write was needed for the facility, and verbally explain the AAT program to the administrators, faculty and parents. The volunteer or therapist does not have to "reinvent the wheel" as he can use the reproducible book appendices to educate all involved in the AAT program, along with referring to the goal and treatment ideas.

As the author, I hope I have provided you with invaluable information regarding using your certified therapy dog as a treatment modality in the treatment of children with autistic spectrum disorder. I have given you necessary knowledge to begin a canine AAT program development with specifically designed for children on the autistic spectrum; and an extensive amount of activities to meet the child's individual and group goals.

I would like to end this book by saying that many "normally" developing children have a positive response to dogs, and children with special needs are no different. I feel that the child on the autistic spectrum has a real connection with Vicki. Perhaps they may not verbalize it, yet their overt reactions to Vicki are unique and playful. Each child has their own way to approach Vicki …some run up to her, smile, pet her, hug her, and want her leash.

Oh, here we go again! Vicki is nudging me…and she would like to end this book by telling one of the experiences we have encountered during our AAT sessions.

Take it away, Vicki!

****

Vicki's Story:
The first time I met this 5-year-old boy, he moved right past Renee and came right to me. He looked me straight in the eye and spoke to me in excruciating and enthusiastic detail about his Disney car shirt. I learned all the characters, the colors, the story, etc. Then he gave me a great big hug and then asked Renee my name. I must say I was honored to hear him speak to me because he does not speak to humans very often. I suppose he was attracted to me because he loves dogs and likes the feeling of my fur? Well, whatever the reason, I really enjoyed his company and he seemed to enjoy mine.

Another one of my therapy friends likes to approach me at his own pace at his own time. "That's cool". I found him very interesting. Initially, he started circling me in about a five foot radius, slowly closing in to a four, three, two, then one-foot radius. It felt like I was being circled by a shark and then I heard the Jaws music playing. Just kidding (Hee Hee). Anyway, then he sat down, took a good look at me and with his closed hand he gently patted me on the head. With the help of the special education teacher, he then opened his hand to pet me. Toward the last five minutes of one of our class group sessions, I started to respond very slowly to Renee's commands. It actually took me about three times for Renee to say lie down before, I did. Renee got the hint I was tired and we ended the session. However, the children found my slow –to- respond behavior very funny and started chanting:

"Vicki's not listening!" Vicki's not listening!".

This is a common saying in the classroom that the special education teachers say to the children. I must say it was funny and all the humans begin to giggle. I would have giggled if I could but I was laughing inside. These are just some of the many adventures Renee and I have experienced. I am sure there will be many more amusing stories to tell. I would like to say good luck. I hope you have enjoyed the book and you pursue working with us wonderful canines. We are fun! You humans are also very amusing.

****

Hello, it is Renee again –thank you Vicki! I have had a wonderful experience in every aspect of becoming a certified therapy dog handler, from choosing a dog to successfully completing an AAT program. It seems that during each therapy session everyone involved has a great time; and the children's goals are being achieved. The positive changes in the child's behavior with autistic spectrum disorder, from the beginning to the end of the session, are keenly observable. The rewards of being involved in an AAT program with children on the autistic spectrum are endless!!!!!!!!!!

APPENDIX A

Prior to Lecture to Facility Personnel

Prior to the presentation, make sure you and your audience has the following handouts to discuss in lecture:

- o Animal Assisted Therapy Dog Presentation (Appendix B)

- o Canine Animal Assisted Therapy Individual Session Protocol (Appendix D)

- o Canine Animal Assisted Therapy Group Session Protocol (Appendix E)

- o Responsibilities of Treating Staff and Animal Assisted Therapy Dog Handler in Therapy Sessions (Appendix F)

- o Autistic Canine Animal Assisted Therapy Program Referral (Appendix G)

- o Canine Animal Assisted Therapy Sign Up Sheet (Appendix H)

Lecture to Facility Personnel
Animal Assisted Activities (AAA) vs. Animal Assisted Therapy (AAT)

Animal Assisted Activities
* provides opportunities for motivational, educational, recreational, and/or therapeutic benefits to enhance quality of life.
* is delivered in a variety of environments by specially trained professionals, paraprofessionals, and/or volunteers, in association with animals that meet specific criteria.
* role of the dog and its handler is to "meet and greet" adults or children in a variety of environments.
* environments may include nursing homes, psychiatric hospitals, medical hospitals, and schools. During these visits, the content is spontaneous or a previous utilized activity can be repeated.
* The volunteer does not have to provide detailed notes or keep a formal client log as there are no specific goals to meet.

Animal Assisted Therapy
* is a goal-directed intervention in which an animal that meets specific criteria is an integral part of the treatment process.
* is directed and/or delivered by a health/human service professional with specialized expertise, and within the scope of practice of his/her profession.
* is designed to promote improvement in human physical, social, emotional, and/or cognitive functioning [cognitive functioning refers to thinking and intellectual skills].
* is provided in a variety of settings and may be group or individual in nature.
* This process is documented and evaluated.

Key Features of Animal-Assisted Therapy:
* AAT is goal-directed.
* There is a specific end in mind, such as improvement in social skills, range of motion, verbal skills, and attention span.
* Any visit with an animal may result in the achievement of one or more of these goals.
* The goals are established and monitored during the treatment session.
* Each documented session goes into the person's record with the progress and activity noted.
* Animal Assistive Therapy is in my words is "Using a certified therapy dog as a creative therapeutic modality to assist autistic children to improve their individualized treatment goals".

I will focus only on the studies I have found specifically regarding Animal Assisted Therapy and Autistic children.

Research on Autistic Children and Animal Assisted Therapy

Although many studies regarding the benefits of animal therapy are documented, I will focus only on the studies I have found that specifically target AAT and children with autism.

Redefer & Goodman (1989) studied twelve autistic children who displayed an immediate increase in social interaction when the dog was present.
   a. The children displayed a decrease in autistic-like behaviors such as hand flapping, spinning and humming; and increase in social behaviors such as interaction with the therapist by joining in, imitating, and initiating activities.
After a one month follow up without the dog and with an unfamiliar therapist, social interaction skills declined; however, they remained above the baseline results.
   c. The authors attribute this improvement in social behavior not only to the presence of the dog, but to the therapist's ability to assist the child in facilitating play, sustaining an activity, broadening his responses, and learning to communicate with the dog.

Martin & Farnum (2002) analyzed behavioral and verbal skills of ten children with Pervasive Developmental Disorder (PPD) using a non-social toy (ball), a stuffed dog, and a live dog.
   a. Overall, with the live dog present, the children laughed more, gave treats to the dog, displayed a more playful mood and increased energy, focused on the dog, initiated numerous conversations and exchanges with the dog, engaged in discussions with therapist regarding the dog, were more apt to agree with the therapist and were less inclined to disregard questions from the therapist.
   b. These researchers conclude that there is a positive behavioral and verbal effect on children with PDD.

On the website http://www.hamline.edu/instech/honors/erin_farrell.pd a research study called The Effects of Animal Assisted Therapy in Children with Autism completed by Erin Farrell, at Hamline University investigated the use of animal assisted therapy dog with autistic children in a school setting; specifically investigating Social Understanding, Social Commutation and Social Interaction.

   a. Data collection was taken on each child in an AAT environment and in a non-AAT environment. The results revealed that an AAT environment for autistic children in a school system facilitated social communication, interaction, participation and initiation of communication.

The website http://youtube.com/watch?v=nHbXVxheEL8&feature=relate, provides excellent videotape presentations of a therapist treating an autistic child in a Canine Animal Assisted Therapy Program.

ASK THE AUDIENCE: *What do you think may be some general benefits of Animal Assisted Activities and Animal Assisted Therapy?*

General Benefits

Empathy
An autistic child may have difficulty understanding the feeling and emotions of others.
   a.   An animal (dog) may help the child in learning to be empathetic to parents, siblings, and classmates.
   b.   The child sees the animal as a peer; hence, it is easier to teach the child to be empathetic with an animal than with a human.
   c.   The child can learn to read an animal's body language, which will possibly carry over to daily life experience with people.
   d.   The child may be able to interpret the animals' feelings, as animals are straightforward and "live in the moment."
Outward Focus
Children with autism are frequently self-absorbed.
   a.   An animal (dog) can help the child focus on his surrounding environment, as he can watch, talk to, or about the animal.
Nurturing
Because autistic children may a display a multitude of weaknesses, nurturing skills may be difficult for them to learn.
   a.   An autistic child can take care of animal during the session. The child can get the dog food and a drink to encourage nurturing skills.
Rapport
Due to the autistic child's socially communicate issues; rapport with others may be difficult.
   a.   The animal (dog) may help ease transition. In a non threatening and emotionally safe environment, the dog may facilitate communication between child, therapist, handler and classmates.
Acceptance
A child with autism may have had negative experiences in which they did not receive a children or adults approval.
   a.   An animal (dog) acceptance is nonjudgmental and forgiving.
Socialization
One of the biggest challenges the autistic child has is in the area of social communication.

a. There is more laughter and interaction among residents when an animal visits a facility. This laughter and interaction encourages socialization among other children, teachers, handler, and all others involved in the session including the therapy dog.

Mental Stimulation

    a. The animal (dog) provides mental stimulation because of increased communication, laughter, play and entertainment, along with brightening up the atmosphere.

Physical Contact and Touch

The autistic child may have difficulty with tactile stimulation, which can interfere with his developmental process.

    a.   Perhaps for some children, a dog can give an acceptable warm furry touch that a human cannot provide.

    b.   An animal's touch (dog) may be safe, non-threatening, and pleasant which can serve as a stepping stone to transition touching of other textures and people.

Physiological Benefits

The autistic child may present with a lot of self-stimulatory behavior.

    a.   A dog's presence can be a calming factor for the child. The therapist may want to integrate a slow rhythmic petting activity to facilitate calming of a child.

Children not appropriate for AAT

* Children who are fearful
* Children who are aggressive
* Children who have allergies
* Children who have compromised immune system
* Children who family view animals negatively due to their family or cultural background
* When the family has a concern regarding zoonotic diseases, diseases that can be transmitted between people and other animals particularly if precautions are not taken.

Rules during and after all therapy sessions

* Supervise children to make sure they wash their hands well with running water and soap after touching the dog.
* Do not let the child put his hands or other object in his mouth after touching dog.
* Do not allow the dog to lick anyone.
* Do not allow anyone to kiss the dog.
* Refer to Responsibilities of Treating Staff and Animal Assisted Therapy Dog Handler in Therapy Sessions (Appendix F)

Group and individual treatment options

Individual treatment goals
Physical:
*   Improve fine motor skills
*   Improve gross motor skills/balance
*   Improve motor planning

Language:
*   Increase the ability to make small talk
*   Increase ability to use simple sign language
*   Increase vocabulary
*   Increase the use the PECS system to increase communication.

Cognitive/Educational:
*   Increase attention to tasks
*   Increase the ability to follow simple directions
*   Increase eye contact
*   Increase ability to point to, identify, and say body parts
*   Increase directionality
*   Improve ability to recognize such as shape, size, and color

Sensory Needs:
*   Increase the ability to tolerate tactile stimulation.
*   Improve ability to tolerate proprioception sensory stimulation to increase ability to attend to tasks.
*   Improve ability to tolerate vestibular sensory stimulation to increase ability to attend to tasks.

Activities of Daily Living
*   Increase the ability to drink from a cup
*   Increase the ability to brush his hair
*   Increase the ability to wash his hands
*   Increase ability to dress

Group treatment goals
Socialization Skills:
*   Increase verbal interactions between children
*   Increase participation in a group setting
*   Improve interactions with teachers
*   Improve interactions with dog and dog handler
*   Increase awareness of others

Pretend play/Imaginative play:
*   Increase cognitive flexibility ability to tolerate three small changes in pretend play activity with dog.

* Increase ability to engage in pretend play activity for two minutes with another child and dog.

Group and individual treatment options

Individual Treatment

One child with therapist and dog handle working specifically on this child's goals An individual Special Education, Occupational Therapy, Speech Therapy session

* Refer to Canine Animal Assisted Therapy Individual Session Protocol (Appendix D)

Group Treatment
* one or two children in a theme based activity
* two to three children in a group setting with a particular pretend theme (playing veterinarian)
* a pre chosen two to three child group session. Two to three children in a group working on one specific goal (fine motor skills).
* ·a classroom group session Two to six children in a classroom group treatment (preplanned treatment with handler and teacher working on overall goals of classroom).
* Refer to Canine Animal Assisted Therapy Group Session Protocol (Appendix E)

Treatment times:
* Individual or two-three group treatment sessions are usually fifteen minute sessions
* Classroom treatment session times range from a half hour to one hour

Example of Individual and Group Goals and Treatment
The occupational therapist using the dog as a modality to facilitate the development of skills needed by the child to achieve independent functioning in the areas of self-help, play, and learning.

These goals are listed on your handout.

For example, these goals may be physical in nature to improve fine motor skills

Goals may be:
1. The child will be able to fasten and unfasten the dogs vest and collar independently.
2. The child will be able to open a small bottle, Tupperware container, and zip lock bag independently to feed the dog a treat.

Some activities may be:
1.   Having the child manipulate buckles, clasps on leashes, collars, and animal carriers
2.   Having the child open containers of treats and feeding small pieces of food to the dog

GROUP SESSION EXAMPLE

Classroom Group Session Example 1

1.   The children, teachers, dog and dog handler march following commands. We have used the commands of "sit", "down", "stay", "sleep", "roll over", "happy dog", "sleepy dog", "sad dog", and "angry dog (I will hold up Vicki's teeth to demonstrate).

2.   Each child chooses a string animal. If the animal has four legs like Vicki, child places animal on the string.

3.   The dog handler gets the dog to wag its tail. The children imitate the dog's movement and then state what emotion they think the dog is expressing; for example happy, sad, or angry.

4.   The child draws and colors the dog in one of the displayed emotions (i.e. happy, play dog), then draws his face with that same emotion.

Documentation
Client documentation should be addressed to all rehabilitation members to meet the requirement of the facility and for reimbursement.
Whatever documentation format is utilized must meet the requirements and re-imbursement criteria of the chosen facility.
The Delta Society Standards of Practice (1996) suggest that the treating thera-pist utilizing the therapy dog document:
- long term goals
- short term goals
- periodic re-evaluation
- goal modification
- adoptive interventions
- methodology used
- identify ways to measure treatment progress

How to refer a child for the AAT Program:
- o   Refer to Autistic Canine Animal Assisted Therapy Program Referral (Appendix G)

- o Refer to Canine Animal Assisted Therapy Sign Up Sheet (Appendix H)

Either split the audience into their health professional disciplines or into a mixed group of professionals, rehabilitation aides, etc. Give out, via handout or verbally, some pre-chosen individual, or group goals.

Each group or discipline group must come up with several activities pending on the goals they were given. These activates will be demonstrated by each group with one health care professional as the leader, with the dog, and dog handler.

Give the audience participants about ten minutes to come up with idea for the goals. Then the health care professional demonstrate there ideas.

Ask are there any questions?

APPENDIX B

Animal Assisted Activities (AAA) vs. Animal Assisted Therapy (AAT)

Animal Assisted Activities
provides opportunities for motivational, educational, recreational, and/or therapeutic benefits to enhance quality of life.
is delivered in a variety of environments by specially trained professionals, paraprofessionals, and/or volunteers, in association with animals that meet specific criteria.
role of the dog and its handler is to "meet and greet" adults or children in a variety of environments.
environments may include nursing homes, psychiatric hospitals, medical hospitals, and schools. During these visits, the content is spontaneous or a previous utilized activity can be repeated.
The volunteer does not have to provide detailed notes or keep a formal client log as there are no specific goals to meet.

Animal Assisted Therapy
* is a goal-directed intervention in which an animal that meets specific criteria is an integral part of the treatment process.

* is directed and/or delivered by a health/human service professional with specialized expertise, and within the scope of practice of his/her profession.

* is designed to promote improvement in human physical, social, emotional, and/or cognitive functioning [cognitive functioning refers to thinking and intellectual skills].

* is provided in a variety of settings and may be group or individual in nature.

This process is documented and evaluated.

Key Features of Animal-Assisted Therapy:
*   AAT is goal-directed.

* There is a specific end in mind, such as improvement in social skills, range of motion, verbal skills, and attention span.· Any visit with an animal may result in the achievement of one or more of these goals.

* The goals are established and monitored during the treatment session.

* Each documented session goes into the person's record with the progress and activity noted.

Research on Children with
Autistic Spectrum Disorder, and Animal Assisted Therapy

Martin F., & Farnum J. (2002). Animal-Assisted Therapy for Children with Pervasive Developmental Disorders. Western Journal of Nursing Research, 24, (6), 657-670

Redefer, L.A., & Goodman, J. F. (1989). Brief report: Pet-facilitated therapy with Autistic Children. Journal of Autism and Developmental Disorders, 19, (3), 461-467..

http://www.hamline.edu/instech/honors/erin_farrell.pd a research study called The Effects of Animal Assisted Therapy in Children with Autism

The website http://youtube.com/watch?v=nHbXVxheEL8&feature=relate provides excellent videotape presentations of a therapist treating an autistic child in a Canine Animal Assisted Therapy Program.

General Benefits

Empathy
Outward Focus
Nurturing
Rapport
Acceptance
Socialization
Mental Stimulation
Physical Contact and Touch
Physiological Benefits

Children not appropriate for AAT
* Children who are fearful
* Children who are aggressive
* Children who have allergies
* Children who have compromised immune system
* Children who family view animals negativity due to their family or cultural background

- When the family has a concern regarding zoonotic diseases, diseases that can be transmitted between people and other animals particularly if precautions are not taken.

Rules During and After Therapy Sessions
* Supervise children to make sure they wash their hands well with running water and soap after touching the dog.

* Do not let the child put his hands or other object in his mouth after touching dog.
* Do not allow the dog to lick anyone.
* Do not allow anyone to kiss the dog.
* Refer to Responsibilities of Treating Staff and Animal Assisted Therapy Dog Handler in Therapy Sessions (Appendix F)

Individual and Group Therapy Goals

Individual treatment goals
Physical:
- Improve fine motor skills
- Improve gross motor skills/balance
- Improve motor planning

Language:
- Increase the ability to make small talk
- Increase ability to use simple sign language
- Increase vocabulary
- Increase the use the PECS system to increase communication.

Cognitive/Educational:
- Increase attention to tasks
- Increase the ability to follow simple directions
- Increase eye contact
- Increase ability to point to, identify, and say body parts
- Increase directionality
- Improve ability to recognize such as shape, size, and color

Sensory Needs:
- Increase the ability to tolerate tactile stimulation.
- Improve ability to tolerate proprioception sensory stimulation to increase ability to attend to tasks.
- Improve ability to tolerate vestibular sensory stimulation to increase ability to attend to tasks.

Activities of Daily Living:
- Increase the ability to drink from a cup
- Increase the ability to brush his hair
- Increase the ability to wash his hands
- Increase ability to dress

Group treatment goals
Socialization Skills:

- Increase verbal interactions between children
- Increase participation in a group setting
- Improve interactions with teachers
- Improve interactions with dog and dog handler
- Increase awareness of others

Pretend play/Imaginative play:

- Increase cognitive flexibility ability to tolerate three small changes in pretend play activity with dog.
- Increase ability to engage in pretend play activity for two minutes with another child and dog.

Group and individual treatment options

Individual Treatment
One child with therapist and dog handle working specifically on this child's goals
- an individual Special Education, Occupational Therapy, Speech Therapy session

* Refer to Canine Animal Assisted Therapy Individual Session Protocol (Appendix D)

Group Treatment
- one or two children in a theme based activity
- two to three children in a group setting with a particular pretend theme (playing veterinarian)
- a pre chosen two to three child group session. Two to three children in a group working on one specific goal (fine motor skills).
- a classroom group session Two to six children in a classroom group treatment (preplanned treatment with handler and teacher working on overall goals of classroom).

* Refer to Canine Animal Assisted Therapy Group Session Protocol (Appendix E)

Treatment times

Individual or two-three group treatment sessions are usually fifteen minute to half hour sessions.

Classroom treatment session times range from a half hour to one hour.

Example of Individual and Group Goals and Treatments

Individual session

Notes:

Group session

Notes:

Documentation

Use the documentation format that meets the requirements and reimbursement criteria of your facility.

The Delta Society Standards of Practice (1996) suggest that the treating therapist utilizing the therapy dog document:
· long term goals
· short term goals
· periodic re-evaluation
· goal modification
· adoptive interventions
· methodology used
· identify ways to measure treatment progress

How to refer a child for the AAT Program

Refer to Autistic Canine Animal Assisted Therapy Program Referral (Appendix G)

Refer to Canine Animal Assisted Therapy Sign Up Sheet (Appendix H)

APPENDIX C

Name

Address

Phone number

E-mail

Administrator's name

Title

Name of program

Address

Date

Dear name of person,

Thank you for the opportunity to educate your staff about the benefits of Canine Animal Assisted Therapy. The immediate positive response observed with dog's name, in both group and in individual sessions, demonstrates how dogs can help autistic children reach their therapy goals.

Enclosed are dog's name Therapy Dog Certification, Basic Obedience Certificate and updated vaccination records.

I will be available to meet on _____, or at another mutually convenient date and time, to continue the development of a Canine Animal Assisted Therapy Program. Please contact me at your earliest convenience.

Sincerely,

Your name here

APPENDIX D

CANINE ANIMAL ASSISTED THERAPY

INDIVIDUAL SESSION PROTOCOL

PURPOSE: The Canine Animal Assistive Therapy Program (AAT) is designed to utilize a certified therapy dog as a therapeutic modality in meeting an autistic child's treatment goals.

TREATMENT SESSION: A child, a health care professional or special education teacher, a certified therapy dog, and a dog handler will be in the individual treatment session. The length of the session will vary depending on the child.

CRITERIA:

1.   The child cannot display aggression toward animals or others.

2.   The child must not be allergic to the dog.

3.   The child must not be afraid of the dog.

4.   The child must not have a compromised immune system.

5.   The parent must sign the facility consent form.

6.   The child's parents must be aware of AAT precautions and safety issues.

7.   Everyone in the treatment session must adhere to the facility's safety policies, rules, and regulations.

GOALS: Goals will vary depending on the abilities of the child with autism. Several goals are listed below. However, AAT goals are not limited as the therapist can establish additional therapeutic goals.

ACTIVITES: Activities will vary depending on the child's abilities. Some examples of activities may include:

Physical:
·   Improve fine motor skills
·   Improve gross motor skills/balance
·   Improve motor planning

Language:
· Increase the ability to make small talk
· Increase ability to use simple sign language
· Increase vocabulary
· Increase the use the PECS system to increase communication.

Cognitive/Educational:

· Increase attention to tasks
· Increase the ability to follow simple directions
· Increase eye contact
· Increase ability to point to, identify, and say body parts
· Increase directionality
· Improve ability to recognize such as shape, size, and color

Sensory Needs:
· Increase the ability to tolerate tactile stimulation.
· Improve ability to tolerate proprioception sensory stimulation to increase ability to attend to tasks.
· Improve ability to tolerate vestibular sensory stimulation to increase ability to attend to tasks.

Activities of Daily Living
· Increase the ability to drink from a cup
· Increase the ability to brush his hair
· Increase the ability to wash his hands
· Increase ability to dress

ACTIVITES: Activities will vary depending on the children abilities. Some examples of activities may include:

Playing Dress Up:

· Play Dress-up: Have the child place a hat on the dog and then child can place his own hat on himself. Continue tasks with other clothing items.

Basic Activities of Daily Living skills (also known as ADL's):

Feeding Skills:
* Give the dog a drink from his bowl, and then the child takes a drink from his cup.
* Give the dog a drink from his bottle, and then the child takes a drink from his bottle.

Grooming Skills:

* Brush the dog with dog brush and then child will brush his hair with his own brush.
* Wash the dog's face with washcloth then the child will wash his face with his own washcloth.
* Wash the dog's paws, and then wash your hands.

Hand and fine motor skills:
* Have the child manipulate buckles on therapy dog's vest, clasps on leashes, and collars.

Language:
* Have the dog follow simple commands by using sign language or speech ("come", "sit", "stay", "stop", "up", and "look").

* Use the Picture Exchange Communication System (PECS) with dog treats, colors, or a dog sitting.

APPENDIX E

CANINE ANIMAL ASSISTIVE THERAPY
GROUP SESSION

PURPOSE: The Animal Assisted Therapy (AAT) Program is designed to utilize a certified therapy dog as a therapeutic modality in meeting treatment goals of children with autism.

GROUP TREATMENT SESSION: The group treatment session will include two or more autistic children, with a combination of an individual therapist, special education teacher, a teacher's aide, a dog and dog handler. A group session may also involve a classroom of children. Parents are also welcome to attend group sessions.

CRITERIA:
1. The child must be able to follow simple commands.
2. The child must be able to attend to an activity for up to _____ minutes.
3. The child cannot display aggression towards animals or others.
4. The child must not be allergic to the dog.
5. The child must not be afraid of the dog.
6. The child must not have a compromised immune system.
7. The parent must sign the facility's consent form.
8. The child's parents are aware of AAT precautions and safety issues.
9. Everyone in the treatment session must adhere to the facilities safety policies, rules, and regulations.

GOALS: Goals will vary depending on the children and group level. AAT group goals are not limited as the therapist can establish additional goals depending on the children's needs.
Physical
*   Improve fine motor skills
*   Improve gross motor skills/balance
*   Improve motor planning

Language:
*   Increase the ability to make small talk
*   Increase ability to use simple sign language
*   Increase vocabulary

* Increase the use the PECS system to increase communication.

Cognitive/Educational:
* Increase attention to task
* Increase the ability to follow simple directions
* Increase eye contact
* Increase ability to point to, identify, and say body parts
* Increase directionality
* Improve ability to recognize such as shape, size, and color

Sensory Needs:
* Increase the ability to tolerate tactile stimulation.
* Improve ability to tolerate proprioception sensory stimulation to increase ability to attend to tasks.
* Improve ability to tolerate vestibular sensory stimulation to increase ability to attend to tasks.

Activities of Daily Living
* Increase the ability to drink from a cup
* Increase the ability to brush his hair
* Increase the ability to wash his hands
* Increase ability to dress

Socialization Skills:
* Increase verbal interactions between children
* Increase participation in a group setting
* Improve interactions with teachers
* Improve interactions with dog and dog handler
* Increase awareness of others

Pretend play/Imaginative play:
* Increase cognitive flexibility ability to tolerate three small changes in pretend play activity with dog.
* Increase ability to engage in pretend play activity for two minutes with another child and dog.

ACTIVITIES: Activities will vary depending on the children abilities. Some examples of activities may include:

Playing Dress Up:
> Have the child place a hat on the dog and then child can place his own hat on himself. Continue tasks with other clothing items.

Basic Activities of Daily Living skills (also known as ADL's):
Feeding Skills:
· Give the dog a drink from his bowl, and then the child takes a drink from his cup.
· Give the dog a drink from his bottle, and then the child takes a drink from his bottle.

Grooming Skills:
· Brush the dog with dog brush and then child will brush his hair with his own brush.
· Wash the dog's face with washcloth then the child will wash his face with his own washcloth.
· Wash the dog's paws, and then wash your hands.

Hand and fine motor skills**:**
· Have the child manipulate buckles on therapy dog's vest, clasps on leashes, and collars.

Language:
· Have the dog follow simple commands by using sign language or speech ("come", "sit", "stay", "stop", "up", and "look").
· Use the Picture Exchange Communication System (PECS) with dog treats, colors, or a dog sitting.

Socialization skills: Activities listed below

Pretend/Imaginary play: Activities listed below

ACTIVITIES: Activities will vary depending on the children abilities. Group activities work on many goals at a time. Some examples of activities may include:

Example of two to three children small group activities:

MR. POTATO HEAD – This activity improves the ability to take turns, communicate, identify body parts, follow directions, point, socially interact, and lengthen attention span. Initially, the therapist may pass out Mr. Potato Head's body parts (i.e. arm). Then the therapist will ask the child to point or touch his arm, then point or touch the dog's arm, and then place the arm into Mr. Potato Head.

COLOR AND TREAT GAME –This activity improves the ability to identify colors, socially interact, take turns, and sign. The therapist will ask a child to pass out colored cups. Then she will ask another child in the group to place a dog treat into everyone's cup. Then the therapist will show, call, or sign a color and the child who has that color will give the dog a treat.

PLAYING TWISTER – This activity improves the ability to: communicate, identify colors, take turns, follow directions, and increase eye contact. One child in the group spins and shows, signs, or calls out the color. The dog, with the handler, sits on the appropriate color. Then the next child in the group takes his turn.

THEME-BASED IMAGINITIVE PLAY
Examples of a two to three children group that is theme based for imaginative play.
*   Have a picnic with the dog. The child and therapist set out the tablecloth, animal plates, cups and napkins, pretend food, feeding the dog treats and a drink, etc.
*   Play doctor. Have the child check the dogs' and therapists' ears, nose, and heart using a plastic medical kit.
*   Dog grooming day (washing, and brushing dog).

CLASSROOM ACTIVITIES
An example of a classroom activity
 The children, teachers, dog and dog handler march following commands. We have used the commands of "sit", "down", "stay", "sleep", "roll over", "happy dog", "sleepy dog", "sad dog", "angry dog" (For instance I will hold up Vicki's teeth to demonstrate angry).

Each child chooses a string animal. If it has four legs like Vicki, place the animal on the string. The dog handler gets the dog to wag its tail. The children imitate the dog's movement and then state what emotion they think the dog is expressing (i.e. happy).

APPENDIX F

RESPONSIBILITIES OF THE TREATING STAFF
AND ANIMAL ASSISTED THERAPY (AAT) DOG HANDLER
IN THERAPY SESSIONS

Responsibilities may include but are not limited to:

Responsibilities of the treating staff:
The therapist should:
- guard against the child physically harming the dog.
- protect the child (watch for signs of stress).
- document activities and progress in the child's AAT goals file.
- come prepared with specific goals in mind and activities to reach these goals.
- observe and monitor the child's responses during the AAT treatment session and modify activities, if needed, to reach specific goals.
- document progress in the child's record and modify goals as appropriate.
- end a therapy session if and when appropriate.
- adhere to the facilities safety, policies, rules, and regulations.

The Responsibilities of AAT Dog Handler:
The dog handler should:
- guard against the dog harming the child.
- protect the dog (watching for signs of stress).
- ensure that the dog clean and well groomed.
- follow the appropriate treatment suggestions of the therapist.
- end the session if appropriate.
- adhere to the facilities safety, policies, rules, and regulations.
- make sure the dog has all vaccinations and routine physical examinations

APPENDIX G

AUTISTIC CANINE ANIMAL ASSISTED THERAPY PROGRAM REFERRAL

Child's name: _____ Age _____ Room _____

Professional Referring _____

<u>Treatment Options (circle)</u>

<u>Small group treatment</u>:   2 to 3   children

<u>Individual Treatment</u>:   Occupational Therapy   Physical Therapy

Speech Therapy   Social Worker

<u>Full Classroom Treatment</u>

Therapeutic goals:

_____ Gross Motor/Motor Planning   _____ Fine Motor/ Motor Planning

_____ Sensory   _____ Language

_____ Communication   _____ Cognitive

_____ Educational   _____ Activities of Daily Living

_____ Social skills   _____ Pretend Play

_____ Other _____

Goals should be limited to 2-3 per session.

Therapeutic Goal Example:

Long Term Goal (LTG): John will make eye contact with therapist 10 times during a 15 minute Animal Assisted Therapy session.

Short term Goal (STG): John will make eye contact with therapist 4 times during 15 minute session).

Data Collection method: Count the number of times eye contact made with therapist?

Goal 1:

LTG:

STG:

Data collection method:

Goal 2:

LTG:

STG:

Data collection method:

Sample form for data collection

Child _____

Date of Service: _____

Activities: _____

_____

Times child made eye contact with therapist _____

Child _____

Date of Service: _____

Activities: _____

_____

Times child made eye contact with therapist _____

Child _____

Date of Service: _____

Activities: _____

_____

Times child made eye contact with therapist _____

APPENDIX H

CANINE ANIMAL ASSISTED THERAPY SIGN UP SHEET

TIME	CHILD'S NAME	TYPE OF TREATMENT
9:00-9:30 AM	Jane Doe	One on One OT Session

RESOURCES

American Psychiatric Association. (2000). Diagnostic and statistical manual of mental disorders (4th ed.). Washington, DC: *American Psychiatric Association*.

Anderson, M. (2007). *Tales from the Table*. London, UK & Philadelphia, PA: Jessica Kinsley Publishers.

Ayres, J. A. (2000). *Sensory Integration and the Child*, Los Angeles, CA: Western Psychological Services.

Bernard, S. (1995). *Animal Assisted Therapy: A Guide for Health Care Professionals and Volunteers*. Tyler, TX: Tyler Press.

Bernard-Curran, S., Cathcart, S., & Scoggin, L., (2008). Review of DVD program Selecting and Training a Therapy Dog.

Buchanan, S. M., & Weiss, M. J. (2006). *Applied Behavior Analysis and Autism: an introduction*. Ewing, NJ COSAC.

Burch, M. R. (2003). *Wanted: Animal Volunteers.* New York, NY: Wiley Publishing, Inc.

Cusack, O., & Smith, E. (1984). *Pets and The Elderly The Therapeutic Bond.* Binghamton, NY and London, UK. The Haworth Press.

Delta Society. (1996). *The Human-Animal Health Connection Animal-Assisted Therapy Standards of Practice.* Bellevue, Washington: Delta Society.

Fine A. H. (2006). *Handbook on Animal-Assisted Therapy: Theoretical Foundations and Guidelines for Practice.* New York, New York.

Fredrickson-MacNamara, M., & Butler, K. (2006). Characteristics of Animal Assisted Therapy/Activity in Specialized Settings. A. H. Fine (Eds.), *Handbook on Animal-Assisted Therapy: Theoretical Foundations and Guidelines for Practice.* (pp. 263-285). New York, New York. Elsevier.

Gammonley, J., Howie, A. R., Kirwin, S., Zapf, S. A., Frye, J., Freeman, G., & Stuart-Russell, R. (1997). Delta Society: *The Human-Animal Health Connection Animal-Assisted Therapy Therapeutic Interventions.* Bellevue, Washington: Delta Society.

Granger, B. P., & Kogan, L. R. (2006). Characteristics of Animal Assisted Therapy/Activity in Specialized Settings. A. H. Fine (Eds.), *Handbook on Animal-Assisted Therapy: Theoretical Foundations and Guidelines for Practice.* (pp. 263-285). New York, New York. Elsevier.

Greenspan, S. I., DeGangi, G., & Wieder, S. (2001). *The Functional Emotional Assessment Scale (FEAS) for Infancy and Early Childhood.* Bethesda, MD: Interdisciplinary Council on Developmental and Learning Disorders.

Greenspan, S. I., Wieder S., & Simons, R. (1998). *The Child with Special Needs Encouraging Intellectual and Emotional Growth.* Reading MA: Perseus Books.

Kamioka, H, Okada, S. Tsutani, K., Park, H., Okuizumi, H. Handa,S., Oshio,T. Park, S-J., Kitayuguchi, J., Abe, T., Honda,T., Mutoh, Y. Levinson, B. M. (1962). *The dog as a co-therapist. Mental Hygiene,* 46, 59-65.

Kamioka, H., Okada, S., Tsutani, K., Park, H., Okuizumi, H., Handa, S., Oshio,T., Park, SJ., Kitayuguchi, J., Abe, T., Honda, T., Mutoh, Y., *Effectiveness of animal-assisted therapy: A systematic review of randomized controlled* trials. Complimentary Therapies in Medicine (2014) 22, 371-390.

Martin F., & Farnum J. (2002). *Animal-Assisted Therapy for Children with Pervasive Developmental Disorders.* Western Journal of Nursing Research, 24, (6), 657-670.

Miller, A., & Chretien, K. (2007). *The Miller Method: Developing the Capacities of Children on the Autism Spectrum.* London, UK and Philadelphia, PA: Jessica Kinsley Publishers.

Morrison, M.L., Animal-Assisted Interventions: 2012, University of Delaware

Pichot T., & Coulter M. (2007). *Animal-Assisted Brief Therapy A Solution Focused Approach.* New York, NY, London and Oxford, UK: The Haworth Press.

Redefer, L.A., & Goodman, J. F. (1989). *Brief report: Pet-facilitated therapy with Autistic Children,* Journal of Autism and Developmental Disorders, 19, (3), 461-467.

Silvia, K., Correia , R., Lima, M., Magalhaes.,A., and deSousa,L. *Can dogs prime autistic children for therapy? Evidence from a single case study.* The Journal of Alternative and Complementary Medicine. 2011, Vol.17, Number 7, pp 655-659.

Stewart, L. A, Chang, C.Y., and Rice, R. Emergent Theory and Model of
Practice in Animal-Assisted Therapy in Counseling. Journal of
Creativity in Mental Health 2013, 8:329-348.

Yeargin-Allsopp M., Rice C., Karapurkar, T., Doernberg, N., Boyle, C. &
Murphy C. (2003). *Prevalence of Autism in a US Metropolitan Area*,
289, (1), 49-55.

.

ONLINE RESOURCES

~**The Activity Idea Place: An Early Childhood Educator's Resource**. http://
www.123child.com/act

~**The American Kennel Club** www.akc.org

~**The Affects of Animal Assisted Therapy and Autism**
http://www.hamline.edu/instech/honors/erin_farrell.pdautism:. (n.d.). *The
American Heritage® Stedman's Medical Dictionary*. Retrieved April 22, 2008,
from Dictionary.com website: http://dictionary.reference.com/browse/autism

~**The Center for Disease Control (2007) Autism Developmental Disabilities
Monitoring: Prevalence of Autistic Spectrum Disorders (ASDS) in
multiple areas of the United States, 2000 and 2002**. http://
www.cdc.gov

~**Autism Society of America.** www.**autism-society**.org/

~**Autism and ABA Introduction to the CCBS Applied Behavioral Analysis
for Autism**. Green, G. Retrieved April 7, 2008 from: http://www.behavior.org/
autism

~**Companion Animal Parasite Control** (www.capcvet.org.)

~**Delta Society.** www.**deltasociety**.org/

~**The Effects of Animal Assisted Therapy in children with Autism.** Retrieved April 5, 2008. Farrell, E. http://www.hamline.edu/instech/honors/
erin_farrell.pd

~**The Greenspan "Floor Model"** http://www.coping.org/intervention/
floortm.htm

~**The Miller Method** http://www.millermethod.org

~Scott, Pat. (2003). **Pat Scott Training School: Canine Stress Signs.** Retrieved February 4, 2008 from: http://www.k9webs.com/patscott/stresssigns.ht

~**Therapet Animal Assisted Therapy** www.therapet.co

~**Therapy Dogs International** www.tdi-dog.or

~**Videotape of Autistic Child being treated with Animal Assisted Therapy**
http://youtube.com/watch?v=nHbXVxheEL8&feature=relate,

ABOUT THE AUTHOR

Renee Farneti Jensen was in the process of publishing this book when she passed away on August 11, 2011 after seven years of battling cancer. During the seven long years of her suffering, she never stopped working and was dedicated to helping children on the autistic spectrum to live a better life. Her determination in helping people with physical, sensory and cognitive disabilities to be independent in all areas of life was her passion. She understood children and their love for animals and learned different techniques in helping children on the autistic spectrum using a therapy dog. Her niece Amy Bennett, who was a certified therapy dog trainer, gave her and her daughter, Aleacia, a trained therapy dog named Vicki. The results were amazing!

Renee was always a perfectionist, and after high school continued her education. She obtained a Bachelor of Science in Occupational Therapy from Syracuse University's Utica College, and a Master's Degree of Art in Education from Seton Hall University. She had over twenty-one years of experience as an occupational therapist and served as a board member of New Hope Assistance Dogs, Inc., Warren, Pennsylvania. As a published author, Renee was both a certified pet therapist and therapy dog owner who developed and implemented a canine animal assisted therapy program in a private day school for children on the Autistic Spectrum. Over the last five years of her life, she focused her career on training and utilizing her certified therapy dog Vicki, as well as writing and working with the children.

Renee was raised in Eynon Pennsylvania, a small town near Scranton, Pennsylvania; and had moved to Scotch Plains, New Jersey with her husband, ten-year old daughter, two dogs, a cat, a hamster and a frog. Now her daughter is 20 years of age and shares her mother's passion for helping people. She is in her third year of school at Purdue University.

www.ingramcontent.com/pod-product-compliance
Lightning Source LLC
Chambersburg PA
CBHW040933030426
42336CB00006B/65